The Other American Governments

Tribal Governments in Transition from Dependency to Sovereignty

Zia Meranto

Metro State University of Denver

www.kendallhunt.com
Send all inquiries to:
4050 Westmark Drive
Dubuque, IA 52004-1840

DEDICATION

Human existence flourishes when people share their goods with one another, when individuals consciously give away more than they take. To have more than what one needs, is an embarrassment, not a sign of success. Phil Meranto, 1939-1985.

CONTENTS

PREFACE

I started writing this book primarily in response to questions I had on how to integrate American Indian politics with courses in American politics, particularly at schools that did not have multicultural, ethnic, or indigenous studies. I was heavily saddened that during my own undergraduate studies only once did any of my classes mention anything about Native people, and that was in Howard Zinn's book, A *Peoples History of America*. More importantly, the class that required Zinn's book was an introduction to American politics. Dr. Phil Meranto, who later became my husband, taught the class. Unfortunately, Phil passed away in 1985, but his passion and perspectives about American and Native politics continued to guide me and heavily influence my academic studies.

By the time I entered graduate school I was keenly aware of the many historical conflicts between the U.S. Government and American Indians. Even though there was an increase in tribal sovereignty, in large part because Indians demanded it, one contemporary issue caught my attention—the Navajo/Hopi "land dispute." Following Phil's lead on reacting to injustice, I quickly became involved in attempting to stop the relocation of the Navajo and Hopi people, a consequence of the 1974 Settlement Act. Other students, faculty, and community supporters felt as strongly as I did, and we soon created an organization called the Big Mountain Support Group. The focus of the support group was to bring elders from the area involved in the "land dispute" to the Denver/Boulder area. In their own voices, the elders told large audiences of the devastation they were experiencing. It was obvious to many of us that the relocation of Indians, similar to the first Indian removal in Georgia in 1830, was done under the pretext of protecting Indians once again. With the removal of indigenous people from their resource-rich land, Peabody Coal Company could quickly step in and develop the coal. In 1987, I wrote my master's thesis on this issue, entitled *The Political Domination of Native Americans: A Case Study of the Hopi/Navajo Land Dispute*. A prior graduate student of Phil's, Dr. Larry Mosqueda, was the chair of my thesis and helped me tremendously on this project. Larry's wife, Patty, edited my thesis. Larry and Patty, Dr. Dennis Judd, Dr. Matthew Lippman, and many others provided me comfort after Phil's passing, and supported me throughout my academic pursuits. After finishing my master's thesis, I pursued my Ph.D. I realized early on that literature on Native rebellion did not exist in the social movement literature; it was as if the 72-day siege at Wounded Knee in

1972, which shared the cover of the *New York Times* with the debacle of President Nixon, never really happened. Had scholars viewed this rebellion as an aberration, or was it too complex for American social movement theorists to tackle? While many books had been written on other American movements, specifically the Labor Movement, Civil Rights, Chicano, and Women's Movement, none had been written on the American Indian Movement. Peter Matthisen's book, *In the Spirit of Crazy Horse,* chronicles the story of Leonard Peltier and the FBI's war on the American Indian Movement; however, distribution of the book was interrupted for almost a decade and was not distributed until 1993. Therefore, I knew what the topic of my dissertation would be.

I had just finished reading one of Ted Gurr's books entitled *Why Men Rebel.* I became inspired and decided I wanted to study with him. When speaking with Dr. Gurr, I told him of my interest in writing my dissertation on the American Indian Movement. He responded that the little he knew about the movement was that it was leaving the streets and entering the courtroom, and encouraged me to pursue my goal. He agreed to be chair of my dissertation. I entered graduate school once again with a well-designed plan. With Dr. Gurr's guidance, the guidance of Dr. Larry Dodd, and specifically the guidance and assistance of Dr. Anne Costain, who wrote *Inviting Women's Rebellion: A Political Interpretation of the Women's Movement*, I finished my dissertation. I appropriately entitled it *The Rise and Expansion of the Native American Movement*; "expansion" because I wanted to examine Native strategies as they entered the United Nations' arena. In 1998, Dr. Anne Costain invited me to write an article for her edited book on social movements. The article, *Litigation as Rebellion,* was published in Social Movements and American Political Institutions. Obviously, Dr. Ted Gurr and Dr. Costain continued to inspire me. I deeply appreciate the theoretical underpinning of why men, women, and now Indians rebel because of their contribution to my education.

In 1992, when I joined the faculty in the Political Science Department at Metropolitan State College of Denver (now a university), I created a Native American Politics course. Before my arrival, Metro had established African American Studies and Chicano Studies, but owing to low enrollment, they had "withered away." Metro then created the Institute for Intercultural Studies directed by Dr. Ali Thobhani, where I taught Native American Politics. After a couple of years of teaching, my dean and chair at the time, Dean Foster and Dr. Norman Provizer, spoke with me about creating a major in Native American Studies. I told them that I thought a minor would be successful but not a major. I was concerned that a department of Native American Studies might well fall by the wayside as had numerous African American and Chicano studies across the nation. Therefore, I suggested that I create a program as a minor, and leave it housed in the political science department. Since the school was not funding the program and since the school was not providing course release time for me to work on the program, there would not be any financial reason to cut the program. Moreover, I believed, and still do, that the numerous cultures we have in the United States should be integrated with traditional disciplines. That is to say, American politics should incorporate the politics of Native nations, ethnic groups, and women. Nonetheless, I have been very fortunate that our students value the courses in Native American Studies. The program has proven to be a much-needed and popular area of study.

While creating the program, however, the task seemed overwhelming; there were only a couple of programs in the nation. Despite my initial feelings, I had a handful of Native students in my classes that encouraged me and made it seem possible. Some of these students were pursuing a degree in political science, specifically Sarah EchoHawk-Vermillion, Pawnee, whose father John EchoHawk started the Native American Rights Fund in Boulder, and Raymond Foxworth, Navajo, currently a Ph.D. candidate. These students and others helped tremendously with creating the minor and with the initial writing of this book. In addition, I must thank all of the people who helped me learn and those who included me on their journey to learn, specifically Dr. Mary Ann Watson with whom I published, adjunct professor Melissa Ortiz, and all of my students, Native and non-Native, that continue to teach me so very much.

Friends and colleagues played a significant role as well. I am grateful to my colleague and friend Rebecca Salinas, who helped me with the cover of the book, used the manuscript in her classes, was a great listener, and provided me with so much moral and emotional support. Gail Garcia, the administrative assistant for our department, provided me with emotional and technical support. Moreover, as I wrestled with the mechanics of how to write this book, I received outstanding support, comments, and suggestions from Dr. Robert Hazan, Dr. Norman Provizer, and Dr. Amy Eckert. A portion of my interest in American Indian politics is rooted in my own experiences, specifically the institutionalization of Indian children. All of the homes I lived in were homes that were heavily steeped in white Christian fundamentalism. Consequently, when I write of the Christianization of Indians, it is not something of which I can be totally objective. This experience affected me significantly, not only in my academic life but in my personal life as well. My choices in life, similar to other children and adults, are often not of my own choosing. I discovered my past had less to do with the actions of my parents or of me, and largely to do with underlying issues of history, racism, economics, and specifically the dictates of cultural transformation.

Consequently, while I am an academic, this book has a strong activist tone. This is why Dr. Elizabeth Cook-Lynn's work resonates so well with me. She is not apologetic about being an academic, activist, and a tribal nationalist, the combination of which makes her work authentic and dynamic. Therefore, while I try to emulate her work, the genius of her writing skills cannot be matched. Take for instance what she writes in *Anti-Indianism in Modern America: A Voice from Tatekeya's Eart*h: "Today, America's tongue is cloaked in ignorance and racism and imperialism as much as it was during the westward-movement era." She says she is not a political scientist, but if one is a conscious Indian, one cannot freely float down the mainstream; politics is in your DNA.

I learned from so many writers, including Elizabeth Cook-Lynn, that objectivity is often nothing more than conformity to mainstream bias. When I strayed from contesting the prevailing orthodoxy, my work seemed inauthentic. I spoke with some of my Native and non-Native students about this dilemma, and they said I should be writing for them, not for academics, and that the tone of my work, coupled with my experience and passion, made my work more accessible to them. That was all I needed to hear. I attempt at every level to include an indigenous perspective, which rarely fits the dominant paradigm that is taught, and rarely challenged. If some people find the indigenous perspective offensive, they should try to determine with what they are offended. Does one really learn if cognitive dissonance is not experienced? Most of what I have learned has come from Native Americans, Navajo Code Talkers, elders, spiritual leaders, Native writers, Native students, and the young generation of Native and non-Native scholars.

Some of these young scholars and academics used portions of this manuscript in their classrooms and gave me valuable suggestions, and for that I thank them. Consequently, I have had time to work out the kinks. But "finished products" are rarely finished. The (tribal) government-to-(federal) government relationship, viewed as fictitious by many scholars, requires continual monitoring. However, when Kendall-Hunt decided to publish my book, I had to let it go, knowing that my mission to provide the basics of Native politics was accomplished. Other more accomplished authors such as Stephen Cornell, Sharon O'Brien, David Wilkenson, David Wilkins, Elizabeth Cook-Lynn, the late Jack Forbes, and, naturally, the legendary Vine DeLoria, Jr. provide a much more in-depth perspective of Native issues and politics; and I thank them for that.

In conclusion, I wish to acknowledge the staff at Kendall-Hunt for their encouragement and support with this project. I hope that it will inspire students to want to learn more about *The Other American Governments*. I often recite to my students the following adage: if you know one country, you know no country. I must add if you know one American government, you know no American government.

INTRODUCTION

It may be that Americans will have to come face to face with the loathsome idea that their invasion of the New World was never a movement of moral courage at all; rather, it was a pseudoreligious and corrupt socioeconomic movement for the possession of resources (Cook-Lynn 1996, 33).

America's love of the American Indian ebbs and flows. At times, Indians are regarded with affection, particularly when they fit American society's historical image of the passive stoic traditional "Red Man." At other times, Americans quickly distance themselves from the original inhabitants, particularly when Indians attempt to reverse repressive and vacillating federal policies; for a rebellious Indian reminds Americans of a past they have yet to embrace. Still many Americans have an undying interest, albeit confused, in American Indians and tribal governments.

How Americans view Indians has largely to do with what they know and what they have learned about them. Some Americans see Indian societies as primitive, traditional, close to the earth, possessing a way of life that respects the planet; but what do they know about tribal governments? For example, do Americans see Indians as American citizens or members of tribal governments? Are they ethnic groups with minority interests or minorities acting as nations? Furthermore, which institution or groups of institutions have the right to control tribal affairs? Should states, various federal government agencies, or tribal governments govern tribal governments? Some of these contradictory representations of Indians expose the ambivalence inherent in American attitudes toward Indians. Unfortunately, Americans demonstrate they know very little about the politics of Indians and Indian nations. Moreover, most American students want to study and learn about the culture and ceremonies of Indians. However, we cannot understand the culture and ceremonies of Indians unless we recognize that culture, land, and politics are intertwined. There are numerous treaties, statutes, executive orders, court decisions, agency ruling, tribal interests that all have a significant role to play in the day-to-day lives of Indians. Moreover, the *trust responsibility* of the federal government states that the federal government has a "duty of protection" toward Indians. Thus, Indians *trusted* the federal to keep its promises to protect Indians in exchange for their land. This relationship is known as a *trust responsibility; a relationship to the United States that resembles that of a "ward to his guardian"* (Cherokee Nation v. Georgia 1831); this is why it is important to connect politics with issues relating to Indian nations.

When teaching American Indian studies, instructors often hear some of the following comments from their students: Why can't we just study the culture and ceremonies of Indians? Why do we have to know so much about Indian politics? Why is the history of Indians so sad? Why are white people to blame? Many of these questions demonstrate a reluctance on the part of students to form a critical interpretation of their government, which is to be expected.

In order to avoid such questions, it would be easier for instructors to address only the culture of the population and leave to conjecture how cultural change occurred without including factors that contribute to that change. However, historical honesty and the reality of American Indians in the twenty-first century suggest that the culture of Indians significantly changed with European contact, and more directly with the creation of the United States. Prior to the European invasion, Indian culture was tied to land. Indians, as practitioners of land-based religions, believed that land was equal to being Indian; not so for early Americans. Americans believed (and still do) that land equaled freedom. Thus, the more land Americans acquired, the more freedoms they believed they acquired. Consequently, Native land would have to move out of the hands of Indians and into the hands of whites. Therefore, federal Indian legislation set in motion Indian land dispossession very quickly, largely to meet the needs and desires of the first immigrants.

Therefore, to discuss Indian culture without understanding Indian politics is to ignore the reality of what it means to be Indian and what it means to be American. It was Euro-Americans, not Africans, not Asians, and certainly not American Indians, who orchestrated the loss of large amounts of Indian land and thus changed Indian culture. To ignore information because it is "too political" is to have an incomplete understanding of what it means to be Indian. This would be like trying to understand what it means to be Jewish without examining the effects of their holocaust. How different are American students from those German students who want to disavow the actions of their government? We must not ignore the consequences of the holocaust in a Jewish Studies program any more than ignore the holocaust in a Native American Studies class.

Subsequently, the increased complexities and actors in tribal affairs, coupled with the increased politicization of tribal governments and Indians, make it even more urgent to understand how American Indian politics work. American Indians are citizens of the United States *and* members of Indian tribal governments. This unique dual citizenship requires that Indians interact with federal and state governments as well as their tribal governments. Moreover, the increased political participation of Indians and tribal governments in both American and tribal politics has made it necessary to know exactly how these governments function, and how they interact with American politics and larger society.

In this text, I demonstrate how in the last decades the interests of American Indians have become increasingly involved with the interests of Americans in a variety of ways. These features, plus others, make American Indian politics exciting as well as ambiguous. Consequently, our analysis must examine multiple levels of power. We cannot examine the interrelated power struggles between Native and non-Native U.S. citizens alone but also the power struggle between numerous governments, bureaucracies, and corporations. Let us start by attempting to create a clear interpretation of history, however difficult this may be.

First, we must accept the fact that the first people to narrate the history of Indians within Euro-American society were non-Indians. Unfortunately, the world did not hear the Indigenous voice until well into the mid-twentieth century. This suggests that the early history of Indians lacked not only Indian participation but also Indian credibility. Keeping Indians in the past and excluding their participation in American history was important to do in developing the new American national character. The purpose of this history was first to introduce and teach certain cultural values and then to put in place a political order that would further those cultural values.

Some of the questions that come to mind regarding this process are, what are the values of this history, what culture was imposed and sustained, what political orders do they represent, and with what ferocity and intensity have they been created and maintained? In answering these questions, we need to examine both the U.S. federal government and American tribal governments; to examine only the former would show a bias that matches much of what history books already portray about Indians. Similarly, to examine the latter without comprehending and applying the unique federal status of Indians within American politics would tend to serve a disparate purpose and mission. It is virtually impossible to get a clear and complete grasp of

American tribal governments without discussing American politics in general, and specifically tribal politics. A history of American democracy has not excluded the influences of European theorists, nor should it. Nor should a study on American history exclude the influences of the first inhabitants. Since these two peoples met, their ideologies, interests, and cultures have intersected, if not collided, in countless ways. In the headlines below, one can see how some of the interests of tribal governments interact with those of Indians, government, and other key players within American politics

---

MEDIA MESSAGES

"Conservationists Question Maka Treaty"
"Toxic Waste Decree Burns Idaho Tribes"
"Tribal Sovereignty at Supreme Court"
"Donald Trump Wants Indians Out of Gaming Business"

In two of the events portrayed above, American citizens protested the right of Indians to fish whales and gamble, while largely ignoring treaty rights and the absolute power of Congress to grant Indians the right to game and fish. In another of the events, Idaho tribes refused to accept the toxic waste of larger society. A third headline demonstrates that conflicts related to issues of sovereignty necessitate the role of the Supreme Court. Unfortunately, many Americans often react to these news stories with confusion and stereotypes largely because they know very little about federal Indian legislation, and because in the process of politically socializing Americans, ideas and values have shaped the reactions of Americans to Indians. That is to say, reactions and opinions are often formed with little knowledge of Indian treaty rights, tribal sovereignty, or the special federal status held by Indians. Consequently, crucial decisions and opinions become biased and thus have the capacity to escalate conflict among and between key players.

For example, Donald Trump, American business magnate, obviously knows very little about the sovereign rights of tribes. Tribes do have the right to open casinos as long as the tribes have the fortitude to deal with the onslaught of state interests and corporate interests such as Mr. Trump's. The Indian Gaming Regulatory Act (IGRA) passed by Congress in 1988 provides a legislative basis for the operation/regulation on Indian gaming. Many tribal governments oppose Congress interfering with their decision to generate additional revenue through gaming.

However, with corporate interests increasing, the IGRA has the capacity to facilitate gaming rather than interfere with it.

Another confusing and hotly debated issue is terminology. Are the first people of this continent Indian, American Indian, Native American, Indigenous, or Aboriginals? Good arguments have been made for the use of any one of these terms. Each of these terms suggests somewhat different emphases in regard to the American experience, social and political goals, cultural nationalism, or global identity. In addition, diverse tribal members are not always in agreement with the use of these terms. Indians who have a close relationship with their tribe either through enrollment or through heritage often prefer to be identified through their tribal name. In this text, various terms are used interchangeably, paying more significance to the use of these terms in relationship to power. For example, the term "Indigenous" often refers to the original inhabitants of the world. This term is often used at the United Nations or in international politics. The term "Red Power," used during the militant years of the late 60s and 70s and in the early 1800s during the "Red Sticks Revolt," reflects the position of Indians in American politics during particular rebellious periods. Americans are most familiar with the contribution of Columbus identifying the population with whom he came in contact as *In Dios* ("in God). Moreover, the term Native Americans can be misleading because many Americans interpret this as meaning they are native to this country; and the term American Indians may not apply to Native Hawaiians or Alaskan Natives.

These terms, treatment, and comprehension of American Indians demonstrate that American Indians are a diversity of Indian tribes possessing a wide variety of cultural expressions, origins, and traditions. This too clearly makes it difficult to treat Indians as a monolithic group.

The Other American Governments examines the politics of tribal governments, and how tribal governments attempt to meet the needs of their population. On the one hand, Indian politics is not that different from American politics. The fact that many Indian nations have democratically elected governments makes them procedurally similar to the U.S. Government. On the other hand, American Indian politics is quite different. These differences are evident on two levels: distribution of power among the various interests, Indian and non-Indian, and the level of sovereignty claimed by federal, state, and tribal governments.

Many of the above issues are examined in the following chapters. Chapter 1 discusses general information about politics, power, and governing—illustrating how power/politics work in governments. Chapter 2 covers the evolution of Indigenous political philosophy and to what extent contemporary Native Americans incorporate traditional philosophy. This chapter also discusses the Iroquois Confederation and questions its influence on American values and ideas. Chapter 3 is about culture, land, and conflict, touching briefly on how Natives view the world, their place in it, and certainly their responsibility to it. This chapter emphasizes the traditional characteristics of sacred ways in Native North America, realizing that some of the traditions have changed, while many more remain virtually unchanged. Chapter 4 demonstrates how tribal governments and American Indians have become what they are today. This chapter relies heavily on the historical relationship between Indians and the federal government, information that is crucial to any analysis on contemporary Indian issues. Chapter 5 is an observation of the characteristics and functions of modern tribal governments. We examine the extent to which distinctive peoples with various histories and traditions incorporate certain elements of a developed government and society. Like other governments or nations, tribal governments desire self-determination and autonomy. Unlike other governments, tribal governments must cooperate, comply, or challenge the numerous agencies that control them, while being cognizant of the following dominant actors involved in Indian affairs: the Bureau of Indian Affairs (BIA), federal government's primary Indian agent; Congress, who has plenary power (defined as absolute and unlimited) over Indian nations; States, which continue to declare themselves the primary power in deciding what happens within state territories; and a more recent actor, corporations, that wield an incredible amount of economic and political clout in American as well as American Indian politics.

Chapter 6 examines various Indian identities and the processes of reclaiming a tribal identity. Assimilative Euro-American education began more specifically in the late 1800s with the introduction of boarding schools and industrial schools. To ensure the eventual demise of Indians, federal policies broke down any semblance of tribal identity with the use of a "blood quantum" or "degree of blood." Chapter 7 addresses the creation of interest groups and social movements, noting various types of activities used by Indians to increase political power. In this chapter, I explain strategies Indians used and continue to use to shape Indian legislation and increase self-determination of tribal governments. Recent information suggests that Indians have increased knowledge of tribal and U.S. federal structures and are therefore better equipped to play the political game. One example of modifying political tactics is the shift away from protest in the streets to protest in the courts. Litigation has taken center stage.

Chapter 8 addresses the consequences of colonization and liberation of Indian women. The relationship between American Indian men and women changed dramatically and contributed to a higher level of conflict and gender inequality within and outside of tribal governments. This chapter identifies and analyzes factors that gave rise to gender inequality. It also provides some suggestions as to how Indian women achieved a level of equality within their communities while not sidestepping the large issue of tribal sovereignty.

Finally, Chapter 9 speculates on the survival of tribal governments. I examine how tribal governments are better able to maintain a place at the bargaining table with federal and state governments. In this chapter, I examine some contemporary issues and demonstrate how these issues have the capacity to increase tribal sovereignty and meet the needs of the Native populations.

Since the beginning of writing this book, there have been a number of books written by leading Native scholars. I incorporate their ideas throughout this book; my citations and bibliography demonstrate this well.

CHAPTER ONE

POLITICS: POWER, AUTHORITY, AND LEGITIMACY

An Indian is a member of any federally recognized Indian Tribe. To be federally recognized an Indian Tribe must be comprised of Indians. To gain federal recognition, an Indian Tribe must have a land base. To secure a land base, an Indian Tribe must be federally recognized (Jaimes 1992, 133).

Politics is about *power.* Simply defined, *power is the ability to influence another's behavior, getting someone to do something they wouldn't otherwise do.* Power is often measured by resources available to influence the *power brokers*. In politics, these resources are often referred to as political resources. Resources, whether measured in terms of wealth, numbers, ideology, education, or status, provide governments with the capacity for increased power. Within governments, the distribution of power usually involves a relationship between governments and the people they represent. However, for tribal governments the definition, application, and use of power are highly dependent upon additional factors. The power of tribal governments is often negotiated with numerous key actors, all of which try to exert power over tribal governments in an effort to get their respective and sometimes collective interests met. Consequently, the powers of tribal government become highly deluded.

Therefore, unlike American politics, where most of the *politicking* is between people and government, American Indian politics is often between tribal governments and the federal government, largely due to the federal status of Indian Nations. Tribal governments are defined as *sovereign nations,* but not treated as such. Under the special federal status of tribes, tribal nations are forced to confer with the federal government when making decisions about education, infrastructure, jobs, religion, housing, and many other issues within tribal boundaries. Given this unique relationship, it has been difficult to examine not only the power of tribal governments and their capacity to govern, but also their capacity to govern within what is defined as federal and state jurisdictions.

Consequently, the authority, or legitimate power, of tribal governments has always been variable if not questionable. Without authority, political resources do not easily convert into usable power. Without legitimate power, the potential for the use of coercion increases, particularly if authority figures perceive nothing wrong with coercing rather than convincing its population of its rightfulness.

Most tribal governments were "reorganized" in 1930 under the Indian Reorganization Act. Since reorganization was more or less mandated by the federal government, many tribal members may not view contemporary tribal governments as legitimate. Opposition to contemporary tribal governments was made known in the 1960s when many of the demands of militant Indians centered on the removal of abusive and sometimes corrupt tribal governments. For example, the Indian Occupation of Wounded Knee in South Dakota in 1973 was a culmination of numerous grievances against an imposed tribal government gone corrupt. Tribal Chief Dick Wilson was not viewed as legitimate by many tribal members. Thus, he relied on coercion of the population rather than persuasion. Still, not all tribal governments lack legitimacy and consequently authority. Many of them, such as the Lummi, Hopi, and Mohawk, have been able to use authority efficiently and effectively; members view these governments as having a sense of rightfulness and legitimacy.

Power, authority, and legitimacy must be viewed as central to politics, whether about politics on the job, at school, home, or in the case of American Indians on tribal land. Politics, then, is the study of *whom, what,* and *how*; who does the influencing, and what or who is influenced; often referred to as the process of governing.

GOVERNING

Government is largely viewed as the *how of politics*, the implementation of the political process. Many governments, more specifically authoritarian governments, or those lacking a level of participatory democracy, control the process and its influence (or coercion) on the people. Most often, when we examine power of nations, we examine military power. The nation with advanced military power is better equipped to control its own destiny as well as the destiny of other weaker nations. Within Native nations, the level of military power is not a factor, largely because they do not have a military. They do have, however, the right to have a police force. In addition, they have the right to establish a tribal justice system and regulate criminal matters that deal with civil matters such as divorce, personal injury, adoption, and so forth.

The Supreme Court stated in 1978:

> It is undisputed that Indian tribes have the power to enforce their criminal laws against tribe members. Although physically within the territory of the United States and subject to ultimate federal control, they nonetheless remain a separate people, with the power of regulating their internal and social relations. Their right of internal self-government includes the right to prescribe laws applicable to tribe members and to enforce those laws by criminal sanctions (Pevar 1992, 95).

Most governments do two things: 1) they make the rules of the game, setting rules that determine who will get the valued things of a society, and 2) regulate the use of legitimate force to get society to participate, conform, and comply with those rules. In trying to determine how tribal governments accomplish the first part of what governments do, making the rules and parceling out the valued things of a society, the rights of tribal government must be examined. Tribal governments have the right to form a government. In the 1930s, under the Indian Reorganization Act (IRA), more than a hundred tribes chose to restructure their governments. The IRA was implemented to "help tribes modernize" their governments. Each tribe had the power to draft a constitution giving the tribe specific power, although subject to the approval of the Secretary of the Interior. Naturally, this meant that the various constitutions had within them a provision that gave the Secretary of Interior review and approval. Only those tribes that reorganized with the approval of the Secretary of Interior are eligible to receive *certain* federal loans. One can see that this in and of itself limits tribal power.

Tribes with constitutions and other various types of political organizations have rights to determine tribal membership, create tribal courts, and regulate tribal property, domestic affairs, commerce, and trade. In addition, these tribes have the right to fulfill the second part of what governments do, that is, regulating the use of legitimate force to get society to participate and comply with tribal rules.

One of the factors that affect the ability of tribal governments to govern is the ominous hand of Congress. Congress has the ability and power to limit tribal powers in a number of ways. In general, Congress allows tribes to have the same power as state governments to regulate their internal affairs, with some exceptions. Naturally, this minor difference has the potential of diminishing the power of tribal governments. The Reorganization Act, discussed above and more succinctly in a following chapter, demonstrates the consequences of Congress interfering with tribal affairs.

Another method of determining what government does is by examining the level of participation of both government and its population. What determines level of participation is largely dependent on the type of political and economic system. For example, socialist governments play a direct role in who gets what because its economic system is based upon a *planned economy* with a focus on equal distribution of resources. Governments with an ideal capitalist system, based on *private ownership of the economy*, do not directly decide who gets what. A basic assumption of capitalism is that people can get *more* of what they want with *less* government interference. The level of government interference in the market varies from government to government specific to that nation. For example, Cuba still maintains socialism as an ideal, but numerous indicators suggest a level of privatization is slowly occurring. Similarly, the United States embraces a *laissez-faire* (hands-off) government, but history reveals that the U. S. has been distancing itself from the ideas of the free-market since the early 1900s. U. S. government interference in the creation of the minimum wage, the inspection of food and drugs, the implementation of environmental protection laws, and the increasing and decreasing of federal and state taxes, to name a few, illustrate that the U. S. is edging away from a free-market system. Moreover, modern tribal governments appear to be more socialistic in nature than capitalistic; but this too is changing.

A government may determine its level of enforcement (the second task referred to above) in a variety of ways. Obviously, governments prefer that people conform, comply, and participate with its laws voluntarily. If the population is socialized to comply with the needs of government, people will give government the right to act and thus minimize the use of force. Various institutions are the agents of this socialization process and encourage its population to comply, conform, and participate willingly with these rules. If the rule book in the form of a constitution does not give rights to citizens, and citizens view the rule book as legitimate, it is less likely citizens will make demands. Similarly, if governments monopolize with few checks and balances, and their citizens view government as the sole regulator of legitimate force, governments may interpret that as meaning they have authority to do whatever they desire.

Unlike the U. S. government, the legitimate power of tribal governments fluctuates with each level of government, whether state, local, or federal. More importantly, the issue determines the level of power of a tribe. For example, the debate regarding gaming on Indian land provides us with a classic example of the use of power and the array of interests. First, tribes view their right to gaming on their territory as a right of sovereignty, not a given right but an inherent right. Secondly, states believe they have rights that override the sovereignty of tribes. States often point to Amendment 10 of the U. S. Constitution that state they have the right to control territory within their boundaries. Another player, corporate casinos believe their right to make a profit is thus infringed upon when Congress allows tribal governments to operate casinos. Interestingly enough, among all of these beliefs and interests it is often the legitimacy of tribal governments that is the first to be questioned, not the rights of states or corporate casinos. Because of this, many tribal governments have difficulty attaining and sustaining a sense of rightfulness within their populations and outside tribal land. The autonomy and sovereignty of tribal governments are questioned and challenged by their members, federal and state governments, corporations, and American society.

POLITICAL IDEOLOGY

As governments cope with issues within their territory, they must be able to apply some semblance of political power. For tribal governments, political power is often sporadic, largely dependent upon the issue or how people's ideology views that issue. The application of power is guided by a set of values, beliefs, or, as it is often referred to, *collective ideology*. Ideology is, in essence, the paint that paints the picture. An ideology helps us understand (1) how the present social, economic, and political order operates, (2) what is good or bad about this order, and (3) what should be done, if anything. An ideology, then, is a set of guiding principles that helps the governed and government make judgments about a variety of issues.

In terms of public policy, ideology is crucial, for it guides what public policy is and shapes the political agenda. In other words, ideology influences the input (idea) of the political process as well as the output (public policy). In the United States, it is essential to note three key political values upon which that ideology has been constructed: *individualism, materialism, and limited government*. These three values, manifested in liberalism and capitalism, guided the writing of the American Constitution and virtually everything political and economic that followed.

Capitalism is the private ownership of the means of production and the distribution of goods and services set by competitive markets. Capitalism has been referred to as an ideology largely because those individuals who subscribe to capitalism make value-based assumptions about man and their expected results. That is to say, capitalists must make decisions on the use of land, labor, and capital (money) in order to make the market work. Additionally, capitalism has three assumptions: that individuals are by nature self-interested rather than collectively interested, and thus seek to maximize their personal or individual returns (profit motive); that man is by nature competitive; and that the combination of profit motive and competition leads to progress and in the end improves the standard of life. In essence, a free market must focus on achieving a natural harmony between supply (production) and demand (desire.)

While capitalism is the economic ideology in the United States, classical liberalism is the political ideology. Unfortunately, most Americans speak about the two ideologies as if they are inherently dependent upon each other, sort of the hand and glove concept. While the two concepts have become closely integrated, many governments have been very creative in combining various ideologies using concepts of classical liberalism and capitalism.

Like capitalism, classical liberalism focuses on a limited government, individualism, and materialism. Therefore, this type of liberalism implies that a limited government is needed to ensure optimum individual freedoms. The main principles of liberalism are associated with John Locke, a seventeenth-century theorist. His two themes focused on the right of individuals to own and use property as they saw fit, rights primarily defined as property rights and equality. In early America, rights were defined largely as the right to own property and to participate in the market. Today, the definition of *rights* has been significantly expanded to include other rights such as civil rights. In addition, when markets in the U. S. were 95% free, approximately 8% of the population had political freedom, i. e., democracy. As democracy has increased, markets have become less free.

This certainly raises questions as to the coexistence of capitalism and democracy. Unfortunately, few Americans are socialized to question this coexistence. Rather, most

Americans support the tenets of capitalism and liberalism and believe the result of the merging or integration of these political and economic ideologies is democracy. In other words, most Americans believe that democracy is difficult to achieve without a *free* market and that individual *freedoms* are less attainable without a *free* market. Interestingly enough, Indigenous philosophy suggests that there is nothing *free* about American democracy. There is little doubt that early Americans would have achieved the magnitude of freedoms without the decrease of freedoms of the original Americans.

Simply put, European Americans set the agenda of Indian/white relations through their interpretation of political and economic ideologies. These new Americans brought Christianity (Protestantism) with them and many believed that in order to be civilized, people needed to own property and be productive on the land. Additionally, land not owned by Christians was vacant. These were the main concepts of the *Doctrine of Discovery*, a precolonial doctrine that the U. S. Supreme Court has used to guide many, if not all, of its decisions pertaining to Indian sovereignty and rights.

Therefore, in attempting to understand how political ideology guides public policy, it is important to know the concepts that dictate *Indian* policy. While the ideology of tribal governments varies, the ideology that shapes politics on tribal land has historically been shaped by the basic tenets of capitalism and liberalism, heavily rooted in the Doctrine of Discovery. Consequently, the ideas of the new Americans very much determined the kind of political policy or political outcome created in Indian Territory.

POLITICAL OUTCOME

The prevailing political-economic philosophy of early America is reflected in the fundamental procedures and laws of the United States, including federal Indian legislation. Historically, the values of Euro-Americans rather than the values of Indians guided Indian legislation, creating a national identity founded on those values. For most people in other countries, national identity is the product of a long process of historical evolution, involving common ancestors, common ethnic background, common language, and, usually, common religion. For them, national identity is organic in character. This has not been the case in the United States, where since the founding of America, national identity is defined in political rather than organic terms.

In Maldwyn Allen Jones' book (1992) entitled *American Immigration*, Jones states that through the colonial period, many Americans tended to assume that difference of language, culture, and religion would interfere if not prevent the creation and growth of a common loyalty. Such a diverse society required a national identity free of such differences, so U. S. national identity became liberty, freedom, and equality. *American culture is the American Creed.* Here, political principle and national identity are inseparable. What would Americans have in common if it were not for the American Creed?

Two hundred years later, political factors are still at the heart of our national identity. In the 1950s, 85 percent of the American population polled mentioned some aspect of American government when asked about their culture. Compare this statistic with seven percent of Germans, and three percent of Italians (Lipset 1979).

Because of an identification based on political ideals, Americans are less tolerant of different ideas and ideologies. Two Italians, states Lipset, can have different political ideologies, one a Communist and the other a Fascist, and neither would deny the "Italianness" of the other; but in the U. S. to say you are a Communist is to be un-American. In fact, the House of Un-American Activities Committee (HUAC) (1938–1975) created to investigate Americans identified as communists viewed these individuals as disloyal and subversive. To many individuals, identifying yourself through heritage, language, customs, or rituals is also un-American. It is transferring allegiance from a political identity to a cultural identity—and there goes a common loyalty.

How much Americans have in common is somewhat divided. On the one hand, there are individuals who have benefited greatly from the American Creed and naturally embrace it. On the other hand, there are people from any number of cultures who have not experienced much liberty or equality; consequently, they pay less tribute to the American Creed. Once these individuals begin filling the vacuum created by defining themselves in political rather than organic terms, it is difficult to suppress the differences among cultures and people, even though the socialization process encourages such suppression.

In many cases, political terms change rather than the identity. For example, at one time in American history many Americans of African descent preferred the term Blacks and then African American, and other Americans of Spanish descent preferred the term Hispanic, Chicano, and now Mexican American. These terms or identities, while separating the group from larger society, may serve an additional purpose. That is to say, these identities are often efforts to re-create what it means to be American and of African or of Hispanic heritage. Once the term becomes a political lens for which to view and understand politics, it has become more than a cultural identity; it has become a political identity.

For Native Americans, Indians, American Indians, Indigenous Peoples, and so forth, identity became intertwined with politics when Europeans arrived, and more so with Euro-Americans. Prior to European arrival, to be Indigenous was to be steeped in a culture free of a political lens. To understand the cultural genocide that was occurring, Indians created a different lens, a political lens that kept their cultural identity intact. The original Americans have maintained an identity that continues to be rooted in a worldview consisting of a custodial and nonmaterialist attitude toward land and natural resources. This worldview naturally sets American Indians apart from dominant society and apart from American ethnic groups as well.

Consequently, Indian identity, unlike American ethnic or immigrant groups, is both political and cultural, and central to the issue of land. Land has been the root of interactions between Indians and Euro-Americans. The Founding Fathers believed the acquisition of land was a right of all Americans, albeit only for certain Americans, and set out to create a government that valued the right to own property over other rights. To them, land equaled freedom. For Indians, the acquisition of land is not a right but a necessity of their culture. Without land, there is no Indian identity, political or cultural. This is very similar to the beliefs of the State of Israel. Without their land base many Israelis believe they cannot be Jewish. Many Americans understand Jews and their desire for a land base, that particular land base, but, unfortunately, cannot understand this concept as it relates to the first Americans.

A very simple method of determining political culture that largely determines political outcome is to examine the values of people and ask Americans what it means to be an American. According to Seymore Lipset (1996) and many of my students, to be an American is to believe in freedom, liberty, equality, free market, competition, upward mobility, materialism, individualism, etc. The new Americans could not have created an identity inclusive of any one of the European groups, for early Americans differed considerably in dress, language, food, traditions, and ceremonies. Therefore, characteristics often used in other countries to define one's national identity are largely absent when defining what it means to be an American.

This unique political American identity, void of an organic culture, centered around traditions, customs, language, and dress, makes Americans less tolerant of identities developed and defined through a cultural lens rather than a political lens, suggests Lipset. This may be a partial explanation for the creation of the newly hyphenated-American identity. The term American reflects an historical identity that is void of characteristics specific to heritage, whereas the terms African American, Irish American, Mexican American, and so forth provide not only information about the heritage of the person but also some political, historical realities.

In order to understand differences of political ideologies and identities and political outcomes, let us compare a major characteristic of Americans, specifically materialism, with a major characteristic of Indians, spiritualism. There is no doubt that the economic system of America, and consequently American public policy, is highly dependent upon valuing materialism, as stated earlier. The American economy can function sufficiently with a limited number of Americans valuing spiritualism over materialism, but the economy would be highly unsuccessful if the majority of Americans valued spiritualism over materialism. For example, there is little doubt that the American system can accommodate a few Amish who reject technology and a few Buddhists who value meditation over shopping, but the system cannot accommodate the majority of Americans valuing such ideas for very long. It would mean the collapse of a main value. Materialism versus spiritualism is but one example. Add to this difference communal living, extended family (rather than a nuclear family), unique dress, language, food, ceremonies, traditions, and a worldview that suggests traditional people are the caretakers of the earth, not the exploiters, and we have a clash of cultures producing interesting and highly conflicting political outcomes.

Since federal Indian legislation is guided by the ideology of Euro-Americans, not American Indians, the historical conflict was and is inevitable. If tribal governments were able to develop their own legislation based on their own political culture, similar to other sovereign nations without state and federal intrusion, conflict might well diminish. However, since the federal government refuses to recognize tribal sovereignty in many areas and since tribal governments have failed to increase their allegiance to the American ideology, conflict continues. If anything, and because of the increased political consciousness of Indians, the ideology of tribal governments appears to resemble characteristics of both traditional and modern forms of governments. This in turn may lead to less internal conflict but increased external conflict.

There are numerous events that illustrate what happens when politics is driven largely by an ideology that conflicts with, or is ill suited to, Indigenous political thought. The roots of modern tribal governing can be linked to early political thought, while the new complexities of tribal governing can be attributed to the increased interactions between tribal governments and numerous key actors within American society. In short, the conflict between American Indians and Euro-Americans is not unlike the current conflict between Americans and traditional Muslims. The traditions of many Muslims are held together by a religion that often views the West as waging a war against their religion, a war where modern societies will not be content until it has destroyed the "backward civilization." The West needs to discredit remnants of the past and, in essence, destroy those traditions viewed as impediments to its definition of progress. Westerners continue to believe they are creating, as Roger Cohen wrote in *The International Herald Tribune*, "a century that will make a diverse world more unified, prosperous and free than ever before." Unfortunately, Westerners give little thought to what is being destroyed or what is replacing these destroyed traditions.

The following information discusses how one leader tried to balance the interests of a more modern government with those of a more traditional population. This example is not unique to this specific Indian nation. As economic development evolves, political development can lag behind. Thus, certain tribal governments organize themselves to work in the interests of other agencies, governments, and institutions outside of Indian Territory, while neglecting and oppressing the interests of their own people. A modern government trying to function within a more traditional setting has the capacity of creating corrupt political outcomes, as demonstrated in the following example.

Corrupt Leadership

Tribal Chief Dickie Wilson of the Pine Ridge Reservation in South Dakota provides a good example of a tribal chief who abused his power and coerced tribal members. Traditional members charged Wilson with misuse of tribal funds, harassing opposition, and failing to adequately protect the rights and interests of the Pine Ridge population. Allegations were made that he accepted government money while allowing Pine Ridge to have high unemployment, a low annual per capita income, and little if any social services. Wilson went against the majority of the members by being in favor of accepting Claims Commission money for the stolen Black Hills and in supporting the Department of Interior's plan to reduce the Pine Ridge Reservation by 133,000 acres. Many members described him as a puppet of the federal government, the BIA, and the Department of Interior (Matthiessen 1992).

To understand the ideologies of the various tribal governments, it would serve us to form general inferences about Indigenous political philosophy. The following chapter assists us in examining the roots of Indigenous political thought and provides us with an alternative for understanding what may have influenced the early writers of the Constitution.

QUESTIONS FOR DISCUSSION:

1) What is the purpose of government?

2) Identify three key political values of Americans.

3) What is it about capitalism that conflicts with values of Indians?

4) Explain why the term *Indian* is largely a political identity.

5) Identify some factors that have the capacity of facilitating corrupt Indian leadership.

CHAPTER TWO

INDIGENOUS POLITICAL THOUGHT

In the realm of political thought, the Indian probably had a greater influence over civilized society than any other savage race. . . . The Indian, therefore, was a factor of immense importance in the 18th century, far out of proportion to his actual numbers (Lokken 1981).

As early as the founding period, Europeans developed a curiosity about Indians, and admitted, to some degree, that the "savages" were capable of developing a political philosophy. Benjamin Franklin, Thomas Paine, and Thomas Jefferson dared to imitate many of the democratic features of the systems of Indians in establishing the United States. Unfortunately, throughout history the overall acceptance that American history, traditions, ideas, and ideals are distinctively American reinforced the idea that Native Americans played little, if any, part in the making of American democracy. This line of thinking eventually led to the formation of numerous negative connotations and outright misrepresentations of the political philosophy of Native Americans.

If the early founders had associated their democracy with Indians, the process of developing the United States politically and economically might have taken some strange and interesting detours. New immigrants were socialized to comply with Indian legislation, policies of removal, relocation, and in some cases annihilation. Subsequently, any recognition of Indigenous influence on American political philosophy mandated suppression.

The scholarship recently emerging, which focuses on the influence of Native Americans on the writing of the American Constitution and other American ideas, provides a framework for examining Indigenous political philosophy. This scholarship yields valuable information about Native political philosophy, and tells us about the roots of American political thought. For example, in *Exemplar of Liberty*, Donald Grinde and Bruce Johansen provide numerous examples where American Indian symbols and ideas were present in the new emerging American identity, symbols that represent liberty, equality, unity, and fundamental principles such as federalism. The authors clearly demonstrate that American philosophy is really a synthesis of European and American Indian political thought.

Familiarity with European political thought is widespread. What is lacking in the literature is a succinct interpretation of Indigenous political thought. The information that follows illustrates that in almost every tribe, clan, or nation, the supreme authority rested in the people rather than the individual. While many of these tribes have changed in their relationship to each other, and certainly in their level of sovereignty, many of the tribal governments in the United States still include portions of their traditional practices and philosophies. Unfortunately, while the U.S. Federal Government learned and borrowed from the Indians' systems of democracy, when the federal government encouraged reorganization of tribal governments through the Indian Reorganization Act of 1934, these newly reorganized tribal governments became less democratic than they had been originally.

Furthermore, when examining the great empires of the south, the attacks on these southern empires have not left us with much to examine. With the exception of the Maya, and to some degree the Inca, no political philosophy exists to observe in the fallen Aztec Empire. Much of the information on these nations, however, does suggest that they too had political systems rooted in democracy. The following information loosely examines these nations, and focuses specifically on the political philosophy of North American tribes.

DEMOCRACY AND AMERICAN INDIANS

Economists and political theorists have often accepted the notion that populations of a certain stage of economic development have traditionally held apolitical attitudes, attitudes that kept them from achieving any political sophistication, or traditions that kept them at the lowest level of economic development (Huntington 1968; Rostow 1962). This notion suggests that there is a strong correlation between economic and political development. The scholarship that points to the last quarter century when the poor and vulnerable peasant population leaves the confines of the village in search of political activity is often given as a classic example. Peasants suddenly become willing to use politics as a strategy to redress their severe economic conditions. Protests and movements are defensive reactions against threats to existing traditional institutions. This suggests that peasants are not political until the conditions necessitate it (Popkin 1979; Scott 1976).

Since politics centers on actions among a group of people involving influence, and involves the use of power, this may be partially true. Peasants and Indigenous populations in the Americas are increasingly participating in a new and different political world. This does not suggest that they came from a world that was apolitical—quite the opposite. The arrival of the colonizers and their greed for land, gold, slaves, and other resources merely intensified the need for a different political thought, one with which Indians could better defend themselves from total destruction. Eventually, their traditional institutions were unable to stop the new landlord–tenant relations that were evolving as Europeans arrived.

When the New World was "discovered," many tribes in the North Americas had their own form of government and their various political ideas. In almost all cases, each tribe considered itself sovereign. While credit is given to the natural-rights philosophers for developing sovereignty as a political concept in their attack on the theory of divine right to rule, popular sovereignty was practiced by many of the tribes in North and South America. Indigenous societies organized themselves around a society formed by the consent of the individuals, and decisions of peace and war were vested in people or a council. The concept of the individual versus the community is one of the major differences between Indigenous philosophy and the monarchies of the Europeans. Indians lived in a democratic state for centuries prior to the arrival of the Europeans. Furthermore, the Inca, Aztec, and Maya governments displayed many of the same characteristics as the ruling European aristocracies. Certainly, there is no way of telling whether tribes of North America had developed in the same way as their southern counterparts. Yet, despite differences in their development, and their governmental structures, traditional tribal governments shared certain values, ideas of leadership, and styles of decision making (Deloria and Lyttle 1983; O'Brien 1989).

While the nations of the new world ranged significantly in governmental structures, very few distinctions were made between the religious and political worlds. Any decision made politically and religiously was for the main purpose of bringing harmony to things in both worlds. In order to accomplish this, each tribe stressed that their members focus on the needs of the community rather than individual needs. The rights of the individual were never to exceed their duties and responsibilities to the community. This feeling of oneness and distinctness from other groups is illustrated by the custom of Indian tribes naming them with a word or words meaning "the People." For example, the Nez Perce call themselves "Nimipu," meaning "the People"; the Seneca are "People of the Hill"; and the Cherokee refer to themselves as "Ani Yun Wiya," or "Real People."

Small bands and tribes like the Yakima operated with a simple government. Their form of government exuded the purest form of democracy, power flowing upward from the community to its leaders. The leaders governed only with the support of the people. Its society was egalitarian and classless.

Similar to the Yakima in levels of democracy but different because of their nomadic lifestyle, was the Lakota Nation, made up of seven bands. Each band formed its own societies made up of two types: the "Akicitas," or police societies that maintained order, and the "Naca," or civil societies that functioned as tribal councils. This council acted only by consensus on a wide range of issues, from tribal hunts location, mediating conflicts between individuals and families, negotiating with foreign nations, to declaring war. Another important figure in the Lakota and many Indigenous societies was the "medicine man." Medicine men were not only respected for their powers and wisdom, but were also consulted when making important tribal decisions. In all Indian cultures, some more than others, there were no divisions between religions and secular life. Religious beliefs and practices were an integral part of all political and social behavior (O'Brien 1989).

The extreme version of direct democracies was the complex, highly structured government of the Iroquois Confederation. Five Nations founded a federal union in hopes of ending the conflict that existed between the various tribes. The Iroquois source of keeping history, using oral history, fixed the origin date between 1000 AD and 1400 AD. Arthur C. Parker, a Seneca scholar, estimated the date at 1390. In 1710, the Tuscarora Nation was admitted into the league. It was at this time that most historians agreed that the confederacy had been in place for more than one hundred years, long before Europeans developed their own constitution and certainly at a time when the Indian population was described as traditional, according to economists (Parker 1916).

The State of Nature, as described by several critics, implies individuals living outside of society, close to God and close to nature. Most of the Indigenous societies had structures that governed but societies that resembled the state of nature. Under the Iroquois form of government, there were no laws governing accumulation, none limiting travel, or any specific law instructing men to submit to its authority. The laws of the land were strictly procedural on how the Great Council was to operate, rather than a list of rights or instructions on what the government expected of its citizens.

The philosophy of the Iroquois was based on the concept that all life is unified with the natural environment and other forces surrounding the people. The people were united to the environment and to the living things in it. The very idea that one could own land, as the early settlers believed, perplexed the Indians. "The soil of the earth from the end of the land to the other is the property of the people who inhabits it." (Grinde 1991, 161).

Iroquois life was spiritually connected with nature, much like the State of Nature concept. However, the power of one was limited, and was only enhanced when it joined forces with the whole. American Indian governments emphasized honor, duty, and responsibility to the whole. Politics were not removed from any part of the whole, nor did their philosophy dictate and control any part of the whole. Land, culture, politics, and religion were intertwined, and any form of government or philosophy could not disentangle these concepts.

As it turned out, the Great Law of Peace, as it was called was effective in ending much of the bloodshed and became the dominant native military and diplomatic power east of the Mississippi. Furthermore, it became the major negotiating force with England.

The following are some structural similarities between the Great Law of Peace and the U.S. Constitution:

1) Distrust of smaller states dominated by larger ones necessitated a device where one colony could veto the actions of the rest of the body; this veto power was already in place in the Iroquois confederacy.
2) The Great Council was made up of two houses.
3) The Iroquois system consisted of representatives from each nation.
4) A speaker from one of the houses was selected for a day.
5) The Head Chief was symbolic with little authoritative power.
6) Since certain members in the League were more powerful than others, checks and balances were put into the constitution as a safeguard against anyone in the council or against any one of the tribes having too much power (Wallace 1946).

Differences between the documents lie in how the two governments defined the role of government. The constitution of the Iroquois concerned itself less with rights than with duties. A major reason for this is that the rights of the people were so thoroughly entrenched in popular custom that they were taken for granted. Therefore, the constitution of the Iroquois did not see the need to explicitly discuss rights. Cultural differences also played a role in the differences. For example, women elected chief statesmen, and they had impeachment powers (Akwesasne Notes 1987).

The Iroquois Confederation raised the question as to what was the purpose of politics in traditional societies. European ideologies suggest that as societies evolve, people arc not capable of sustaining a level of "free state" as noted in the state of nature. Government thus becomes a necessary evil in order to control man's passions. If this is the case, the Iroquois society had progressed into an interesting combination of a society, bearing all the traits of a free state and a highly developed government. Indigenous societies in the New World had a level of democracy not then realized in any part of the Old World. Paradoxically, by emulating the Iroquois Confederation, the U.S. Constitution provided the mechanisms for political leaders to force a population to conform to the Europeans' standard of democracy.

In 1934, the U.S. Federal Government, having failed to destroy all traditional Indian forms of government, instituted the IRA of 1934. This Act forced those Nations that agreed to the Act to reorganize and become the mirror image of the federal government. The federal government suggested Indian tribes design a constitution, elect representatives, disentangle religion and politics, and bring about a new philosophy toward tribal rights and lands. The purpose of this Act was to organize and, for many, impose an alien form of government on tribal cultures, while clearly eroding traditional tribal governments. How ironic that a system so similar to the Iroquois Confederation would eventually be forced upon the very population whose ancestors created it several hundred years earlier.

DEMOCRATIC EMPIRES OF ANTIQUITY IN THE AMERICAS

The Iroquois Confederation is but one strong example of the evolution of Indigenous political thought. Other examples are the large empires of the Aztec, the Maya, and the Inca in Latin America. While these empires were distinctively different in their political philosophy than their northern counterparts and in many cases to each other, their ideas were still deeply rooted in democracy.

The empires of Aztec, Maya, and the Inca were unlike any form of government that existed in North America. These three empires incorporated previously autonomous, culturally heterogeneous societies into large territories and dominated them. No doubt, these dominant societies exploited resources from the subordinate societies in much the same way as the Spanish colonists upon their arrival. In fact, the very idea that these empires eventually became hierarchal in structure made it easier for the Spaniards to impose their form of servitude.

The political and social institutions of the Aztec and Inca were undergoing continuous change in response to their varying fortunes and their rapid cultural evolution. The earlier kinship neighborhoods and clans possessed considerable democratic qualities. For example, leaders were elected by the general membership of commoners, and advised by a council of elders. They organized themselves in a similar fashion as the clans and communities in North America, and in many ways, they were closer to the democratic system of their northern counterpart, than to systems of Europe at that time (Conrad and Demarest 1984).

Eventually, the imperial ideology offered the promise of greater status and wealth for achievements in war and trade. The formal system of a monarch was not established until about 1370. It was at this time elite monopolization of land and wealth occurred, privileges of dress, and limited ownership and education to the nobles. The state comforted the commoner with the reminder that these decrees were established for the health of the entire states. A cycle of increasing imperialism and class stratification began. The new wealth and power of the military subsequently brought in more tribute, furthering their dominance.

The Aztec and Inca societies evolved into separate centralized political authorities, a landed aristocracy, and a large tribute sector of the economy. Their ideology successfully integrated religion, economic, and social systems into an imperialist war machine. By the time the Spaniards arrived, the economic and social foundations of the empire had been laid. This system proved to be pliable institutions in the hands of the Spanish.

The manner in which the Inca and Aztec organized themselves to ensure the proper use of the land was characterized as oppressive. One portion of the literature on these empires suggests that the totalitarian rule was an unbearable tyranny and that the Spanish conquest actually benefited the people. Another portion of the literature points out that the rule of the Inca and the Aztec was stern and rigorous but just. This literature cites the existence of distinction between different social classes, but marvels at the manner in which the guardianship of government was exercised. Rather than see this as oppressive, the people looked upon this guardianship as something quite natural.

Unlike the Aztec and Inca, the Maya culture is still very much alive in Guatemala and Mexico and for the most part bears many of the same characteristics of the Maya of the pre-Columbian period. Two characteristics that still exist are moderation in all things, and the attitude of live and let live. Also still apparent is a highly disciplined society that believes no one should strive for more than their fair share. Concepts rarely strived for are individualism, equality, freedoms, and liberty. The practice of self-restraint, cooperation, and disciplined work, rather than an individual's work, are key ingredients in a society (Menchu 1983; Thompson 1963).

Similar to the northern indigenous population, the Maya, like the Inca and Aztec, developed devotion to the soil and what it produced. The method of governing prior to the Spaniards' arrival was a loose federation of autonomous city-states governed by a small caste of priests and nobles. A civil ruler was defined as both governor and bishop. Thus, the federation of the southern populations of Central America was similar to the federation of the Iroquois. No matter what the government structures were prior to the arrival of the Europeans, devotion to land and what it produced dictated the type of government. Therefore, it could be said that as land became centrally owned or individually controlled, and as a member's responsibility to the community changed, as it had within the Inca and Aztec populations, the political philosophy of Indigenous tribes began to change as well. When property became a civil right, the role of government changed as well.

Nevertheless, the federations of the Iroquois, Inca, Maya, and Aztec and the smaller federations like the Yakima and Lakota bands were more efficient than other governments of their time. According to Benjamin Franklin, "the councils of the savages proceeded with better order than the British Parliament" (Johansen 1982, 74).

Still, philosophers continued to suggest that the State of Indians was probably the first state of all nations, uncivilized and apolitical. Not dominated by the Spaniards, most indigenous people were in that natural state, "being restrained by no laws, having no Courts, or Ministers of Justice, no Suits, no Prisons, no Governors vested with any Legal Authority," writes Johansen (1982, 88).

There was, however, something intrinsically misleading in the way Europeans viewed the Indian society in respect to the State of Nature. This view was inherently rooted in ethnocentrism. The lack of restrictions put on Indians by their form of government made Thomas Jefferson assume that the Iroquois government was a truly egalitarian form of system and a virtuous order. Jefferson erroneously focused on government and ignored a fundamental part of government, its people. People created government and Indian governments recognized this. Indians were more egalitarian and more virtuous because they had not become greedy, corrupt, or self-centered like Europeans. Was it government's responsibility to create a virtuous society through laws, rights, and procedures? Could leaders who were susceptible to corruption create a virtuous society, particularly when societal values consisted of individualism, competition, and materialism?

While governments often can and do create society, the underlying traits of the people who create government need to be examined. Indigenous political philosophy, or *Indigenism*, does not attempt or pretend to separate religion from politics. At the same time, their philosophy does not include religious proselytizing and economic imperialism, two main characteristics of many modern governments. These two ideas became tools, or weapons, for the mobilization of the people, and thus became increasingly important to the process of government.

When Indigenous governments of the "New World" adopted these two ideas as a strategy of surviving and expanding, they began to portray European societies. This ideology, based on increasing its number of followers and its territory, required the implementation of institutional devices in order to keep it sustained. Paying tribute to supreme rulers and creating a military that was more expansionist than protective occurred. There is little evidence among indigenous ideologies that indicates religion conversion was forced. To the extent that Aztec expansion had an ideological basis, it lay in its economic benefits rather than its religious integration.

The imperialist nature of Meso-American empires has been heavily distorted. Most of the literature agrees that their type of imperialism was one where expansion was a natural consequence of power differences between polities rather than arising from a particular social structure. We do know that warfare greatly shaped their cultures and histories as it has societies throughout the world. We also know that the oppression the Inca, Aztec, and Maya people experienced under the Spanish did not end with the colonial period. To this day, the Maya in Guatemala and Mexico and the Inca in Peru continue to endure very oppressive conditions. The social conditions these populations are forced to experience are intolerable, suggesting that no matter how democratic and independent they were, the democracies of the present have restructured them to resemble their conquerors, leaving fewer traditional democracies to examine.

It has taken more than two hundred years to examine the influence of the first Americans on the U.S. government and the idea of indigenous political thought in the Americas. Since history is written by its victors, this should come as no surprise. The current enthusiasm surrounding the contribution of American Indians in books like Johansen, Grinde, Weatherford, O'Brien, Mohawk, and others may make the topic more palatable for some Americans, but not necessarily any less difficult to swallow. Scholars and publishers are still less inclined to include in literature the role of American Indians in shaping American ideas to the same extent they accept the role of the Greeks, for example, even though many scholars realize Greeks did not corner the market on democracy. As Jack Weatherford (1988, 145) points out, "Greeks who rhapsodized about democracy in their rhetoric rarely created democratic institutions." Most of the Greek cities like Athens functioned as slave societies and were not egalitarian or democratic in the Indian sense. U.S. southern states certainly identified much more with the ideal of Greek democracy based on slavery than with the Iroquois democracy where slavery did not exist. Indigenous political thought and its contribution to the evolution of modern American thinking provides us with much to examine. If Indigenous political thought is excluded, how can American politics be understood? Furthermore, how are we able to understand contemporary American Indians if we do not understand how the two governments historically interacted? The following chapter examines the culture of American Indians, and demonstrates how they are integrated with politics while noting to what extent traditions, values, and culture have become eroded

QUESTIONS FOR DISCUSSION:
1) What are some of the problems that might occur by associating American democracy with that of the Iroquois?
2) Identify three similarities and differences between the U.S. Constitution and the Iroquois Confederation.
3) Where did Indians get their rights?
4) Identify some key differences between the indigenous nations of Central America and those of northern America.
5) What are some of the contributions of Indians to the Americas?

CHAPTER THREE

CULTURE, LAND, AND THE SACRED

In marked contrast to traditional western religions, the belief systems of Native Americans do not rely on doctrines, creeds, or dogmas. Established or universal truths—the mainstay of Western religions—play no part in Indian faith. Ceremonies are communal efforts undertaken for specific purposes in accordance with instructions handed down from generation to generation. . . Where dogma lies at the heart of Western religion, Native American faith is inextricably bound to the use of land. The site-specific nature of Indian religious practices derives from the Native American perception that land is itself a sacred, living being (Justice Brennan 1988).

Unfortunately, Justice Brennan's opinion was a dissenting opinion in the *Lyng v. Northwest Indian Cemetery Protective Association* case. The Supreme Court rejected claims by Yurok, Karuk, and Tolowa Indians that the plans of the U. S. Forest Service to build a logging road through the High Country would violate rights protected under the First Amendment and various federal statutes. The three Indian Nations alleged that the road project would irreparably damage certain sacred sites and interfere with religious rituals that depended on privacy, silence, and the undisturbed natural setting (Deloria, Jr., 1992).

The opinion of Justice Sandra Day O'Connor stated that U.S. economic interests outweighed Indian religious rights. In essence, her opinion states society could destroy sacred sites for economic reasons. This case illustrates that while Indian religions are entitled to the same protection as other Americans under the First Amendment, and certainly by the Indian Religious Act of 1978, economic interests may and often do override this entitlement.

What is interesting about this case, other than the obvious from an Indigenous perspective, is that the logging road was never completed. In 1984, while the case was still pending, Congress passed the California Wilderness Act exempting much of this same area from logging. In 1990, Congress passed the Smith River National Recreation Area Act, exempting the proposed site of the road from construction. For the time being, the sacred areas were largely preserved, albeit not out of any concern for the religious rights of Indians.

As stated eloquently by Justice Brennen's dissenting opinion, prior to the European invasion, Indian culture and land were connected. In fact, many Indians continue to believe that a people without a land base cannot be a people. Consequently, the sacred culture (religion) makes the people.

For Americans it was people or, as Justice Brennan stated, doctrines, creeds, and dogmas that lie at the heart of Western religion; a dogma created by government and a dogma that contributes heavily to the culture of America. Chapter 1 of this text demonstrates how unique early Americans were when they created a national identity, void of many European cultures. Certainly, the early Americans brought with them ideas and values that made up American culture. However, most, if not all, Americans willingly relinquished ideas and values that interfered with their becoming American. Therefore, if religious values protect the earth rather than exploit the earth, either religion or values must change. Thus, early Americans believed that the more land they acquired, the more freedoms they acquired: Land equaled freedom. To fulfill their thirst for freedom, Native land would have to move out of the hands of Indians and into the hands of whites. Consequently, as Indian land became depleted (and freedoms of whites increased), the capacity of Indians remaining Indian became less of a possibility. This was not a coincidence. The implementation of federal Indian legislation ensured to the utmost degree this consequence.

As stated earlier, land-based religions are the opposite of Western religions. "The site-specific nature of Indian religious practices derives from the Native American perception that land is itself a sacred, living being," stated Justice Brennan. "Native culture is inherent in and indistinguishable from specific land and specific geography," Native scholar Elizabeth Cook-Lynn states in her book *New Indians Old Wars* (2007, 121). Here we have a Supreme Court Justice and a Native scholar stating the same thing.

So what is culture? Professor Cook-Lynn cites the late Dr. Alfonso Ortiz, a major Tewa scholar from New Mexico.

> "Culture refers to a system of historically derived meanings and conventional understandings embodied in symbols; meanings and understandings which derive from the social order, yet which serve to reinforce and perpetuate that social order; the intellectual aspects of Indian ideas, rules, and principles as they are reflected in mythology, world view and ritual (Cook-Lynn 2007, 121; Ortiz 1969).

For example, Navajo culture (religion) has a number of ceremonies. Most of these tribal ceremonies mark important changes in an individual's life—birth, coming-of-age, death. Many other ceremonies are performed for healing sickness, renewing relationships with spirit beings, initiating people into religious societies, praying for success in hunting, planting, and growing crops, bringing rain, and giving thanks for the harvest of food. A few of these ceremonies are the Blessingway, Enemy Way, Evil Way, and Life Way.

In 1864, the Navajo (Diné) were forced at gunpoint to go on the *Long Walk* to the Bosque Redondo internment camp. Approximately 9,000 Navajo were forced to walk the 450 miles to the camp. In 1868, the Navajo returned home. Upon their return to their land their worldview, religion, and their social order were reinstated according to instructions given in the sacred stories. Today, as in the past, Navajo, similar to other Indian nations, must go into sacred high places, lakes, and isolated sanctuaries to pray, fast, receive guidance, and train young people in the spiritual life of their community. In these sacred places, native people relate to ancestors, humans, plants, animals, and to spirits. While at Bosque Redondo, the Navajo people were not allowed to practice their religion; federal agents did not allow them to perform their ceremonies. That was neither the first nor the last time Indians were denied their religious rights. The U.S. Commission on Civil Rights noted in 1983 that "over the past three centuries, federal agents have suppressed the practice of 1,000-year-old ceremonies that served a central and life-sustaining function for American Indians" (Hirschfelder and de Montano 1993, 112). The federal government's failure to protect American Indian religion stems largely from the belief that Western religions are superior, and that Indigenous peoples' beliefs, as stated by Justice O'Connor, cannot and should not be protected over economic rights.

Contemporary Indian traditions and ways of worship continue to contain elements of classic tribal oral traditions and sacred ways similar to those practiced by the Navajo. There is no doubt, however, that some of these traditions and sacred ways have evolved and changed in response to poverty, oppression, racism, economic exploitation, and technology on the ecosystems of the earth. Moreover, contemporary sacred ways can and do overlap many different tribal communities. Many of these sacred ways may even contain practices that are not indigenous to this particular Indian community. This portion of the chapter focuses on sacred ways of Native American people in the United States. By simply letting *The People* (Indians) speak we can better understand traditions and sacred ways.

The People have a different "worldview," and it is the difference in worldview that separates Indians from Euro-American, and led to a misunderstanding of each other's cultures. Dr. Ortiz defines the term worldview by saying:

> The notion "world view" denotes a distinctive vision of reality which not only interprets and orders the places and events in the experience of a people, but lends

form, direction and continuity to life as well. World View provides people with a distinctive set of values, an identity, a feeling of rootedness, of belonging to a time and a place, and a felt sense of continuity with a tradition which transcends the experience of a single lifetime, a tradition which may be said to transcend even time. (Ortiz 1973, 91)

Dr. Ortiz went on to explain how religion differs from worldview. A worldview provides people with a structure of reality, while religion provides a people with their fundamental orientation toward that reality. Sacred ways then are guiding visions in common that help people create a structure and deal with that reality.

Many individual Native Americans may not share their traditional, cultural, or ceremonial experiences because they are prohibited from discussing them, or they may fear that non-Indians may develop prejudices and misconceptions as has happened historically. In their effort to assimilate Indians, the federal government decided many Indian ceremonies were illegal, some of which are discussed later in the chapter.

What has been deciphered thus far is that most Native Americans share the following six concepts:

1) A belief in or knowledge of unseen powers; what some people call The Great Mystery.
2) Knowledge that all things in the universe are dependent on each other.
3) Personal worship reinforces the bond between the individual, the community, and the great power. Worship is a personal commitment to the sources of life.
4) Sacred traditions and persons knowledgeable in sacred traditions are responsible for teaching morals and ethics.
5) Most communities and tribes have trained practitioners who have been given names such as medicine men, priests, shamans, caciques, and other names. These individuals also have titles given them by *The People* that differ from tribe to tribe. These individuals are responsible for specialized, perhaps secret knowledge. They help pass knowledge and sacred practices from generation to generation, storing what they know in their memories.
6) A belief that humor is a necessary part of the sacred; the belief that human beings are often weak—we are not gods—and our weakness can lead us to do foolish things; therefore clowns and similar figures are needed to show us how we act and why (Beck, Walters and Francisco, 1977, 8).

A belief in or knowledge of unseen powers is portrayed in various ways. The Hopi and Zuni people dramatize their relationships to unseen powers in the Kachina, dances, in kiva activities, in prayers, songs, legends, and other sources of knowledge about the sacred powers. For other tribes, these mysterious powers are found in objects such as plants, wood, and feathers. Other native people say this mystery is the soul of a person. Dreams and visions are born in the soul or "the spirit" and dances and other ceremonies can restore "the spirit" in the people.

Another common belief is that all things in the universe are dependent on one another. If we believe that human survival is dependent upon maintaining the relationship between animals, plants, rivers, the earth, and so forth, then it is a belief that we will take care of the environment and constantly be aware of how our actions affect other beings. Out of this reality or worldview came the idea (the orientation of that reality) of "seven generations." Simply stated, many oral traditions contain a responsibility of taking care of "Mother Earth" well into the future. That is to say, with every activity today we should stop and think about the consequences of that activity for seven generations. It is through this interdependency and awareness of relationships that the universe is balanced. When there is an imbalance, healing ceremonies are performed and rebalancing is sought.

For example, at the heart of one Navajo healing ceremony is the Blessingway. The Blessingway is a ceremony where balance is restored. Many Native American traditions are concerned with balance and imbalance, harmony and disharmony. For example, before a Dine (Navajo) woman gives birth she may request that a Blessingway be performed for her so that her delivery will be bearable. A Blessingway, or "no sleep," is a one-night sing when a medicine man sings from late evening until early dawn, "until dawn has a white stripe" (The Sacred 1977, 271).

A third concept is the nature of personal and collective commitment, prayers, and other forms of sacred worship. Worship is also a very common practice of Western religions; different are the procedures or rituals used to purify, bless, and sacrifice. In order to purify their body, Native Americans may engage in sweatbaths, smoking, or smudging (blowing smoke of cedar, sage, or sweetgrass on the body). During a blessing, you pray or ask for power and strength. When sacrificing you take something of yourself and willingly give it free of charge. Songs, music, and dance, as in the Sun Dance of the Sioux, the Green Corn Dance, and the Ghost Dance, usually accompany these rituals.

The Sun Dance is a religious rite. Men pierce their muscles willingly sacrificing to experience visions and feel closer to the spirits. The Sun is revered as the highest form of masculinity since it gives Mother Earth life and warmth. The Seminoles, Creek, Cherokee, Yuchi, and Iroquois, as well as other tribes practice the Green Corn Dance. The dance typically lasts for three days for most tribes and includes numerous activities. Thanks are given for the corn, rain, sun, and a good harvest during the dance. In addition, corn is not eaten until the Great Spirit has been given proper thanks.

The Ghost Dance developed between 1869 and 1872, and quickly spread across the nation. The original idea of the Ghost Dance stated that the dead would return and that the end of the world was near. Another aspect of the Ghost Dance, and why it was outlawed by the federal government, was built around the prophecy that by Indians dancing, the world would return to the way it was before whites arrived and Indian ancestors would return. This religious movement reinstated hope for those Indians killed by disease, massacres, and internment camps.

Another tradition that was not allowed was the Potlatches or "giveaways." Giveaways are performed when Indians distribute wealth among their members. This is often a measure of how generous one is. Giveaways are ceremonies to assist others that are in need of financial or material assistance (Watson and Meranto 2001). To early Americans it made little sense to give your "stuff" away. In capitalism, a person is not supposed to give anything of value away; rather they should sell it. Federal agents provided Indians with rations of food or clothing. Indians would share these rations with other Indians. From the perspective of the early Americans, whose values were steeped in individualism and self-centeredness, giveaways made no sense. Consequently, the following letter from a Commissioner of American Indians states succinctly how Indians were to behave:

To All Indians:

Not long ago, I held a meeting of Superintendents, Missionaries and Indians at which the feeling of those present was strong against Indian dances, as they are usually given against much time as is often spent by the Indians in a display of their old customs at public gatherings held by the whites. . . .I feel that something must be done to stop the neglect of stock, crops, gardens and home interest caused by these dances or by celebrations, pow wows, and gathers in of any kind that take time of the Indians for many days. . . .No good comes from your "give away" custom at dances and it should be stopped. You do yourselves and your families great injustice when at dances you give away money or other property; perhaps clothing, a cow a horse or a team and wagon. . . .and to have no drugs, intoxicants, or gambling, and no dancing that Superintendent does not approve. I could issue an order against these useless and harmful performances, but I would much rather have you give them up of your own free will and therefore, I ask you now in this letter to do so. Chas J. Burke, Commissioner (Bureau of Indian Affairs, Circular No 1665).

The letter continues to state that the Commissioner would give Indians one year to show they have changed. If after a year the Commissioner does not see change, "then some other course will have to be taken."

In the next chapter, we discuss "the other course" that was taken, specifically, the General Allotment Act. This Act attempted to create a "healthy selfishness" in Indians. However, this too failed to convince Indians that their ways were heathen and should be abandoned. Giveaways, dancing, and, interestingly enough, gaming would continue to be practiced, albeit underground. Unfortunately, misunderstandings, misconceptions, outright arrogance, and ignorance often led federal agents to disallow Indians their rights to perform their traditions and ceremonies.

Another long-held belief and practice is how Native Americans learn their morals and ethics. In oral traditions, Native children learn how to be patient, unselfish, aware, and respectful of the earth and of others. Elders teach respect for other peoples' ways of worship as well, something the Euro-Americans did not learn or practice. Stories told by elders teach morality and ethics through sacred knowledge.

In every Indian nation in North America, priests, medicine men, caciques, singers, and shamans are responsible for passing knowledge and sacred practices orally from one generation to the next. This knowledge is often secret as well as sacred. During some of the more brutal events such as removal, massacres, the spreading of disease, and the removal of Indian children to boarding schools, some of the secret sacred knowledge may have skipped a generation, been lost, or not remembered. In some cases, sacred practices have changed as Indians of different nations lived together. This is most likely how the Ghost Dance religions and other traditions spread so quickly.

The final concept most Native Americans' traditions share is a common belief that humor is a necessary part of the sacred. The integration of humor into the belief of Indians is a reminder that human beings are often weak and this weakness can lead to foolish things. Therefore, as Dr. Alfonso Ortiz suggests, humor makes things endurable. Death, separation, sorrow, hunger, and other experiences along the *Path of Life* can lead to an imbalance. Clowns and other figures teach us to not take ourselves too seriously, and help with restoring balance. Many of the dances and song festivals are full of drama, joking, and satire. Lame Deer, a Sioux man, states the important role of the clown:

> For people who are as poor as us, who have lost everything, who had to endure so much death and sadness, laughter is a precious gift. When we were dying like flies from the whiteman's diseases, when we were driven into the reservations, when the Government rations did not arrive and we were starving, at such times watching the pranks of a heyoka much have been a blessing (Erdoes 1972, 237).

Many Americans are familiar with the Coyote referred to as a foolish figure. It has become very common to see a Coyote in American paintings and other forms of art without Americans actually understanding the role of the Coyote. The Coyote, Rabbit, and Raven are known to create death, bring light and fire, and tools for survival. Jokes, puns, and satire are important teaching tools. "Fundamentally, the sacred clowns portray the Path of Life with all of its pitfalls, sorrows, laughter, mystery, and playful obscenity" (Beck et al 1977, 297).

Because of the magnitude of Indigenous cultures within the United States, there are a number of areas this chapter will not address. However, I will address many of them in broad terms. For example, Europeans view time as linear, thus conceiving the past as a "long straight road leading backward from the here and now to a distant invisible point on the horizon" (Zimmerman and Molyneaux 1996, 12). Many Indian communities conceive time not as linear but as circular, where time is marked by birth, death, and regeneration. The spawning of the salmon is a key seasonal marker for Indians of the Northwest Coast, as is the harvest of corn for those tribes that perform the Green Corn Dance. In this way, Indians observe a natural calendar whose markers are the changes in the world around them.

Also important for most Indian traditions is the great significance of dreams and visions. "Dreaming is believed to be a source of spirit power, which may be used to gain knowledge and insight or to foretell the future" (Zimmerman and Molyneaux 1996, 130). Peyote was and continues to be used by sacred individuals primarily to obtain visions for purposes of supernatural revelations. Peyotism consists of a belief in existence of power, spirits, and incarnations of power. The religious use of peyote started well before the arrival of the Europeans in Mexico. Peyotism later was adopted by the Plains Indians arriving in North America "when the indigenous people were badly in need of spiritual uplifting and cultural strength" (Fleming 2003, 218), and was largely a result of Euro-Americans to Christianize, civilize, and force Indians into a capitalist system.

Another tradition is the use of symbols and patterns by Native cultures to express their connection with the sacred. Symbols and patterns on everything from baskets, pots, dress, footwear, jewelry, and weaving remind Indians of the religious and secular significance. For example, artists, such as Ted Henry, a contemporary silversmith, tell their stories in silver bracelets. One of Henry's storytelling bracelets depicts a Hogan, trees, the four sacred mountains, sheep, and a herder on horseback. Alita Begay is a weaver, and she weaves one of the earliest of the known styles, a Chief blanket. A Chief blanket today is distinguished by its square shape and by its plain design in blue, red, black, and white (Watson and Meranto 2001).

While there are many differences among the various Native traditions, they all share a common recognition of nature and they are informed by spiritual significance. That is to say, certain creatures and landforms possess a special significance. The eagle, the hawk, the crow, the owl, the muskrat, the otter, the deer, the buffalo, mountains, rivers, bluffs, and rocks all have spiritual significance linked to particular tribal traditions and local geography or characteristics. It is this recognition of sacred places, places where man can come in contact with spiritual forces that lies at the heart of land-based religions. Christians might go to a cathedral or some other man-made structure, for instance, but American Indians commune more closely with spiritual truth at sacred sites. There are so few sacred sites left Indians pray that all Americans will work together to preserve rather than destroy them. While all traditional Native peoples share a reverence for the natural world, this has not been the case for doctrines of Western religions or the ways of contemporary life. The more modern way of life often leaves no room for ancient knowledge or values.

Vine Deloria wrote about tribal religions versus modern technology, and what technology represents in the following statement:

> The important aspect of Indian tribal religions, however, has been their insistence on developing and maintain a constant relationship with the spiritual forces that govern the lives of humans. As ceremonies have lost their content, with the changing of life styles, they have been forgotten or abandoned. The recent efforts of Indian activists to reclaim tribal ceremonies have highlighted the dilemma of today's religious Indians. A traditional Indian finds himself still experiencing the generalized presence of spiritual forces; at the same time he finds himself bound by the modern technology of communications and transportation, which speed his world far beyond its original boundaries (Deloria 1974, 251).

There have been many attempts by contemporary Indians to restore ceremonies, traditions, and practices that have been lost. The concept of Survival Schools is one example. The original focus of survival schools was to maintain the language, the songs, and the respect of the earth of their ancestors. In the late 1960s, Indians became aware that they were under siege, particularly in the urban areas. Native Americans were losing their children to juvenile courts and to state foster care. In 1972, organizers of the American Indians Movement (AIM, discussed in Chapter 7) and parents started their own community school. Organizers wanted to create an educational system that would help Native children never forget who they are.

Over the last 20 years, the tactics of the early survival schools have been introduced in numerous Indian tribal colleges. Today, there are approximately 37 American Indian tribal colleges in the United States. The curriculum at those colleges includes language, culture and ceremonies specific to those tribal colleges. Education has become a tactic of *The People* to resist forced attempts to change their ways of life and the ways they worship. While there is no doubt some of these sacred worships have changed and evolved as Indians have been removed and relocated and faced what appears as insurmountable experiences, many of them continue to be practiced. As Americans attempted to civilize, Christianize, and impose a foreign economic system onto Indians, new Indian strategies emerged. Following is a statement made by a Hopi man of knowledge who reacted to attempts made by missionaries to convert the Hopi man.

> We may be foolish in the eyes of the white men, for we are a very simple people. We live close to our great mother, the Earth. We believe in our God, as you believe in your God, but we believe that our God is best for us. Our God talks to us and tells us what to do. Our God gives us the rain cloud and the sunshine, the corn and all things to sustain life, and our God gave us all these things before we ever heard of your God. . . . Your God is a cruel God and not all-powerful, for you always talk about a devil and a hell where people go after they die. Our God is all-powerful and all-good, and there is no devil and there is no hell in our Underworld where we go after we die. No I would rather stick to my God and my religion than to change to yours, for there is more happiness in my religion than there is in yours (Monsen 1907, 270–271).

Red Jacket, a Seneca leader, told Mr. Cram, a Boston missionary, the following:

> You have now become a great people, and we have scarcely a place left to spread our blankets. You have got our country but are not satisfied; you want to force your religion upon us. Brother; we do not wish to destroy your religion, or take it away from you. We only want to enjoy our own. (Delivered at a Council of Chiefs of the Six Nations 1805) (Parker 1952, 123).

In many cases, the oppressive condemnations stated in this chapter forced Indians to go underground to practice their beliefs. No doubt, in recent times, the United States has become more tolerant of the sacred ways of Natives. However, it has been an interesting process to see how and under what circumstances the 1978 American Indian Religious Freedom Act was passed guaranteeing constitutional First Amendment religion freedom protection for American Indians. While this is a step in the right direction, the question that might be pondered is if America was founded on religious freedoms, what took Indians so long to get their religious freedoms guaranteed. In addition, even though Indians do indeed have religious protections, the case that opened this chapter, the *Lyng v. Northwest Indian Cemetery Protective Association*, demonstrates that land-based religions do not fit nicely into the U.S. economic system or Western religion. In the end, this case is a powerful testament to the cultural survival of Indians, and a story that will be told for generations to come.

In addition to the American Indian Religious Freedom Act 1978, American Indians have also been successful in passing the Native American Graves Protection and Repatriation Act of 1991. The graves protection and repatriation act establishes that Native Americans tribal groups own or control human remains or cultural items that are discovered on tribal and federal lands. Indigenous objects must be returned to tribes upon their request.

A number of statutes and regulations during the late nineteenth and early twentieth centuries effectively criminalized a range of spiritual practices, from the Ghost Dance to the giveaways. Naturally, since many of these ceremonies and traditions are intrinsically connected to sacred land, the loss of land further denies Indians their religious rights. Even with the passage of the American Indian Religious Freedom Act (1978), there lacks any sort of enforcement provisions that support the rights of Indians to practice their ceremonies and traditions, especially if those practices interfere with the rights of non-Indians or use a substance like peyote, which larger society views as an illegal drug.

> In *Employment Division, Department of Human Resources of Oregon v Smith* (1990) usually referred to as "The Peyote Case," Justice Scalia argued for the Supreme Court that ingestion of the mild hallucinogenic substance, peyote, by members of the Native American Church is not an activity deserving of protection under the Free Exercise Clause of the First Amendment of the Constitution (Churchill and Morris 1992, 21).

Rather than outlaw the use of peyote, the Supreme Court decided the American Indian spiritual practices are up to individual states. This does very little to support the religious rights of Indians. The next chapter details how culture, land, and religion were and continue to be political tools of the federal government, especially when it comes to modernization and the economic development of sacred sites. It is by understanding the history of Indian legislation that students see how difficult it is to separate politics from culture

QUESTIONS FOR DISCUSSION:

1. What are the basic differences between the worldview of Christians and the worldview of traditional American Indians? Trace these differences to some historical and contemporary conflicts.

2. How do *Giveaways* clash with the basic concepts of individualism, materialism, and capitalism? Can you identify other beliefs that conflict with U.S. economic practices?

3. Explain the main reasons for passing the American Indian Religion Freedom Act of 1978 and the Native American Graves Protection and Repatriation Act of 1991. Discuss how these acts increase religious rights and tribal sovereignty.

4. What is the role of the clown and jokers?

5. Is there a conflict of interest when the trustee of Indian land and an impartial buyer of that land is the same entity? (The next chapter helps answer this question.)

CHAPTER FOUR

HISTORICAL ANALYSIS

"Men make their own history, but they do not make it just as they please; they do not make it under circumstances chosen by themselves, but under circumstances directly found, given and transmitted from the past" (Marx, printed in Tucker 1978, 595).

The above quotation by Karl Marx suggests that the historical pattern of a group's subjugation shapes their resistance. That is to say, how Native Americans move from *hopeless submission to hopeful noncompliance* is largely determined by the historical realities of the treatment of Native Americans by the U.S. federal government. The historical circumstances of Native Americans, more so than other groups, were created and conditioned by federal Indian legislation, doctrines, dogmas, and creeds. Indian policies written and implemented by non-Indians changed the Indian way of life, but did little to significantly improve it. In their attempt to find the ideal Indian policy, the Euro-Americans developed one vigorous policy after another. If a policy of removal and isolation was impossible to maintain, if Indians could no longer be pushed westward to avoid contact, and if it suddenly became inhumane to conduct wars of extermination against them, the alternative became assimilation. When this latter option also failed to bring about the desired effects, Congress tried other approaches such as reorganization, urban relocation, termination, and a new application of self-determination. It is only within the last twenty years that there has been some consistency in how Congress and presidential administrations interact with tribal governments. This consistency developed largely out of a response to politically active tribal governments seeking increased sovereignty. Politicized tribal governments and American Indians evolved by enduring a precarious and often volatile relationship with the federal government and its administrative machinery, specifically the Bureau of Indian Affairs (BIA).

Historical literature demonstrates that the relationship between Indians and the federal government can be described in a variety of ways: *landlord to tenant*, which focuses on private ownership of land; *father to child*, which describes Indians as historically incapable of taking care of themselves; *ward to guardian*, which adopts the idea that Indians look to the U.S. Government for protection, guidance, and support; and *core/periphery*, which centers on distribution of power between the more developed nations (core) and the less developed, (periphery). However, the legal definition that guides and interprets congressional law, provided by Supreme Court Justice John Marshall in 1830, is that of *domestic dependent nations*. This definition is based on the *ward to guardian* concept, stating that the federal government is the legal guardian of Indians. However, no matter what definition is chosen, one thing is certain: structural inequalities increased between the two groups, and the ward, periphery, child, or tenant became highly dependent upon the guardian, core, father, or landlord, thus creating an ongoing dependency and a vicious cycle difficult to break.

Numerous questions emerge with issues of dependency. Are Native Americans worse off economically because of their dependency than they would be otherwise? Does dependence upon the federal government entail a net loss or foreclose opportunities of greater benefit to the economy of tribal governments? Are US funds exploitive or beneficial? Are Indian nations structurally underdeveloped because they are dependent, or are they dependent because they are underdeveloped? Finally, are Native Americans able to acquire the skills to free themselves from their dependency while in a state of forced dependency on the United States?

The answer to these questions is highly dependent upon the applied perspective. From the Indigenous perspective, federal Indian policies have kept Indians in a position of subjugation with limited power to design their own destiny. From the federal government perspective, federal Indian policies were written and implemented not to necessarily benefit Indians, but to benefit larger society; after all, the Europeans came to the Americas to create a nation consisting of similar people with similar values. Nonetheless, while the manipulation and suffering of Indians may not have been a conscious goal of administrators, the environment and competitive nature of American society fostered policies that increased the inferior position of Indians, and contributed to a life of dependency.

Moreover, federal government continues to assume that as Indians integrate into American life, specifically the American economy, Indian values and culture are replaced by American values and culture, much like it has for immigrating groups. While this has occurred to some degree, what is more noticeable in the various activities of Indians is an interesting and convoluted mixture of the past with the present. Culture, systems, and society evolve as the "dance" continues between Indians and larger society, with the federal government often pulling the strings.

SETTING THE SOCIAL AND STRUCTURAL ARRANGEMENTS

Early interactions between the U.S. government and indigenous people developed through treaties, often referred to as *rational–legal documents*, thus providing an illusion that these documents were free of passion. Early white settlers believed treaties brought about an air of civility and legitimacy in relations with Indians. The first treaty between the various Indian nations and government was in 1778. This treaty was between the United States and the Delaware Nation, and agreed to let colonial troops pass through Delaware territory. In the subsequent century, the United States would enter into six hundred treaties and agreements with Indian nations, many of which were broken or misinterpreted by the federal government. In short, this "civilized method" of negotiation became the accepted strategy of the U.S. government to acquire Indian land and culturally assimilate Indians.

Treaties continued to be a method of transferring land out of the hands of Indians and into the hands of Euro-Americans. Eventually, the decisions of the Supreme Court made it necessary for Congress to participate with the creation of laws that would support those decisions. Legal history underlying the political relationship between Indians and European colonists was shaped by one significant case. In the 1823 case of *Johnson v. McIntosh*, the Court decided that when a non-Indian purchased land from an Indian tribe they had not obtained a valid title. The United States had become the rightful owner of all tribal land by virtue of the European "discovery" of the "new world" and the "conquest" of its people. Therefore, the purchaser of Indian land could not legally "buy" the land the tribe did not own. Aboriginal title possessed by Indigenous peoples granted them merely a "right to occupancy," not a right to sell.

Chief Justice Marshall suggested that discovery (recognizing Columbus as the true discoverer) did indeed give title of the land to the Spaniards. Europeans took their cue from the *Doctrine of Discovery* and *Rights of Conquest.* In simplest terms, these two concepts justified and rationalized ownership of the land in the Americas. Taken from John Locke's philosophy of Natural Law, it held that any Christian, clearly read European, that comes upon waste land, land that was virtually vacant of inhabitants, assumed ownership because it was God's will that such land be put to productive use. Those individuals who laid claim to this land and cultivated it owned it. Marshall's narrow interpretation of discovery gave Europeans the justification to refuse Indians the right to their aboriginal land. His definition, in effect, set the groundwork for land disputes to be defined as a landlord–tenant relationship between government and Indian nations. The Chief Justice not only appointed the federal government as the ultimate landlord with the power to end Indian occupancy on the land, but also gave the landlord the power to control and regulate land use (Cohen 1942). The *Johnson v. McIntosh* Case set a precedent on how government and Indians were to interact in the years that followed.

Shortly after the *Johnson v. McIntosh* Case, Marshall was asked by the State of Georgia to interpret which political power controlled land within Georgian territory. In order for the State of Georgia to acquire new resources (mainly gold), the removal of thousands of Creek and Cherokee Indians would have to be undertaken.

In *Cherokee Nation v. Georgia,* the Supreme Court determined that the federal government held legal guardianship over Indian affairs. Furthermore, if the state needed the land, the state was authorized to remove the Indians (Cohen 1942). Despite the court's decision, many Indians refused to leave. Therefore, under the pretense of protecting both the tribes and the state, Congress passed the Indian Removal Act (IRA). The IRA stipulated the removal of the Indians "for their own protection." Gold was discovered in Cherokee land six days later. Relying on the IRA, the state of Georgia declared that the gold rightfully belonged to the state and began relocating Indians (Foreman 1953).

THE REMOVAL PERIOD

That it shall and may be lawful for the President of the United States to cause so much of any territory belonging to the United States, west of the river Mississippi. . . to which the Indian title has been extinguished, as he may judge necessary, to be divided into a suitable number of districts, for the reception of such tribes or nations of Indians. . . that the United States will forever secure and guaranty to them, and their heirs or successors, the country so exchanged with them: *Provided always*, that such lands shall revert to the United States, if the Indians become extinct, or abandon the same (Getches, Wilkinson, and Williams 1993, 124).

By 1835, the Cherokee Nation cases contained two basic thrusts on the status of Indian tribes: (1) Indians were under the protection of the federal government by virtue of its ward-to-guardian relationship, and (2) tribes possess a certain amount of sovereignty to shield themselves from any intrusion by the states. Additionally, it was the federal government's responsibility to ensure that this sovereignty was maintained (Cohen 1942, 83).

One of the fundamental weaknesses with these two cases was that the federal government was not capable of protecting tribes from state intervention, largely because at that time state militias were much stronger than the federal militia. Deprived of any real protection from invasion, tribes were therefore forced to initiate treaties with states—treaties that may have protected the Indians from physical destruction but that became a method for states to take Indian land.

During the next decade, Judge Marshall was determined to strengthen the definition of the Indians' relationship to the U.S. government as that of "ward to guardian." In his defense of the government intervention, he stated that Indians looked to the government for protection, and relied upon its kindness and its power. Furthermore, Indians were "so completely under the sovereignty of the United States, that any attempt (by foreign nations) to acquire their lands, or to form a political connection with them, would be considered by all an invasion of our territory and an act of hostility" (Deloria and Lytle 1983, 30).

Therefore, Marshall established the framework that made Indians the federal government's responsibility. Despite the unfairness of the use of treaties to settle disputes between Indians and whites, this method was the accepted norm until the 1870s. In 1871, Congress declared Indian nations would no longer be recognized for the purpose of making treaties. The era of treaty-making thus ended. The Ute signed the last major treaty in 1914, thirty-three years after Congress' declaration (Cohen 1942).

The 16,000 Cherokee who walked from Georgia on the "Trail of Tears" were not the only Indians forced to move to western reservations. Many other tribes experienced relocation. For example, the Choctaw gave up 10 million acres east of the Mississippi and moved west. In addition, on March 6, 1864, as many as 9,000 Navajo were removed from their homelands and relocated to the banks of the Pecos River in New Mexico. They were now dependent upon the U.S. Army for food rations. It was in this manner that the federal government was able to preserve its domination of Indians.

The relationship of dependency was maintained and sustained with the creation and implementation of numerous federal policies. Similar to Georgia, states continued to intervene into the affairs of Indians, forcing tribes to seek federal protection against aggressive state actions. This action in turn firmly established a psychological dependency not only in the minds of Indians but also in the minds of whites. By appealing to the federal government to intervene against state aggression, the federal government hoped Indians would view the federal government not as the creator of their situation, but as the rescuer. Consequently, any future encounters or decisions automatically necessitated the involvement of the federal government. This made tribes easier to manipulate, while solidifying their control and intervention. Consequently, dependency as a way of thinking and acting became firmly entrenched in the minds of Indians as well as in the minds of larger society.

Removal and relocation of Indians, however, did not occur solely as a means of increasing the territory of the new Americans. Removing Indians onto reservations ensured, to some degree, that whites and Indians would be separated, thus preventing any real understanding of each other's cultures. Federal government made few efforts to culturally integrate Native Americans whether educationally, socially, or economically. In fact, many of the policies suggest that there were great initiatives on the part of the United States to collectively practice discrimination against the culturally distinct natives. Obviously, had Indians accepted the main principles of American liberalism or been adequately socialized to the needs of the federal government, there may not have been such aggressive legislation.

Liberalism is based on the Lockean view that private property is a natural right and is viewed as the basis of prosperity as well as morality, social equality, and a democratic government. This political philosophy rejected by most Indians promoted the commercialization and appropriation of land. In essence, the interaction between American Indians and whites was based on land, and continued to be the impetus for policy making by the federal government well into the twentieth century. In other words, dependency, removal, and relocation worked to increase the rights, specifically the right to private property, of Euro-Americans, while stripping Indians of their rights to collectively own land. For the early settlers, the creation of reservations and the relocation of Indians onto them became the key to solving the land question.

Economists suggest that had there been genuine efforts on the part of early Americans to incorporate Indians into the American economy, it is less likely removal of Indians onto reservations would have been necessary. Much like early immigrants, Indians would have been more fully integrated into local and regional economies. However, the lack of demand for Indian labor, the refusal of Indians to sell their labor or become slaves, and the increased demand for Indian land played out a different scenario. Around the 1880s, the federal government altered its policies in dealing with Indians. Rather than continue the path of relocation—seemingly impossible because land was needed for railroads, new communities, and industry—government opted for a new approach to the Indian problem, namely assimilation, or, as many Indians refer to it, cultural genocide.

UNITING THE TWO DISTINCT CULTURES

Between 1887 and 1927, Indians saw themselves confronted with a series of new problems. They could now choose to either live in small communities, as many of them were accustomed to, or accept small allotments of land with the possibility of becoming U.S. citizens. If they refused to live on these small allotments of land, their alternative was to move further west in hopes of finding land they could settle without fear of further removal.

In 1887, President Chester A. Arthur believed assimilation was the key to the "nagging Indian problem." He said the answer was "to introduce among the Indians the customs and pursuits of civilized life and gradually to absorb them into the mass of our citizens" (Cohen 1942, 129). Responding to his suggestion, Congress passed the General Allotment Act of 1887 (GAA). There were two main ideas behind the GAA:

> 1) Communal land was savage. White individual ownership would create pride, self-interest, and healthy selfishness, leading to Christianity and civilization.
> 2) This act would make it easier to acquire individual Indian land than to acquire land from a tribe.

As can be seen in the following provisions of the Allotment Act, Europeans believed this backward civilization that did not exploit the fruits of the land, as instructed by God, needed to change, and any traditional modes of thought would need to be destroyed in order for progress to pursue. Moreover, only white individual ownership of land would lead to Christianity and civilization. This raises the question as to the intent of the GAA. If this is the case, why allot land to Indians at all? Maybe in hopes of liquidating Indian land, the very thing it did accomplish.

THE CHIEF PROVISIONS OF THE ALLOTMENT ACT

1) a grant of 160 acres to each family head of 80 acres to each single person over 18 years of age and to each orphan under 18, and 40 acres to each other single person under 18; **2)** a patent in fee issued to every allottee but to be held in trust by the Government for 25 years, during which time the land could be alienated or encumbered; **3)** four years allowed Indians when they should make their selections should be applied to any tribe—failure of the Indians to do so should result in selection for them at the order of the Secretary of the Interior; and **4)** citizenship to be conferred upon allottees and upon any other Indian who abandon their tribe and adopt "the habits of civilized life" (Getches et al 1993).

By 1934, the GAA reduced Indian land from 138 million acres in 1887 to 48 million (Wax and Buchanan 1975, 114). In addition, in 1891 an amendment to the GAA resulted in Indians losing additional land. In the 1891 amendment, the Secretary of the Interior was given the right to lease the land of anyone who, in the Secretary's opinion, "by reason of age or other liability" could not "personally and with benefit to himself occupy or improve his allotments or any part thereof" (Cohen 1942, 130). That is to say, the Secretary of the Interior had dictatorial powers over the use of the allotted land. He and he alone could decide whether the behavior of Indians, after receiving their allotted land, portrayed a "healthy selfishness that would lead to civilization and Christianization."

However, before land was allotted to individual Indians, the federal government would need to know who was Indian. That is to say, in order to distribute tribally controlled land to individual Indians, government needed to determine who was Indian. Consequently, an "Indian identification standard" would need to be implicitly imposed, but explicitly applied in future legislation. The federal government decided an Indian was someone who was at least one-fourth Indian.

If the federal government could set and hold the criteria of who is Indian at the designated one-fourth standard, it was hoped the "Indian problem" eventually would be solved either through assimilation or marriage. More importantly, government hoped that Indians would develop characteristics more similar to those of "true" Americans, values and characteristics that focused on an individual identity free of a tribal identity and tribal control. Incorporation of Indians into U.S. economic and political structures could occur only as individuals. The U.S. national identity is highly dependent upon viewing oneself as an individual rather than as part of a collective. What Europeans failed to understand or ignored is that it is as difficult for Indians to develop a concept of self as it was and continues to be for Americans wrapped in liberalism to develop a concept of the collective.

Naturally, these two distinct processes made the cultural transformation of Indians historically difficult. Consequently, Senator Pendleton, a fervent supporter of allotment, pursued this endeavor in another drastic way by declaring:

> They must either change their mode of life or they must die. We may regret it, we may wish it were otherwise, our sentiments of humanity may be shocked by the alternative, but we cannot shut our eyes to the fact that is the alternative, and that these Indians must either change their modes of life or they will be exterminated. . . .In order that they may change their modes of life, we must change our policy. . .We must stimulate within them to the very largest degree, the idea of home, of family, and of property. These are the very anchorages of civilization; the commencement of the dawning of these ideas in the mind is the commencement of the civilization of any race, and these Indians are no exception (Gates 1979, 11).

It is apparent in the above quotation that the federal government believed a sense of liberal culture needed to be instilled in Indians through the invention of new amendments and policies, for it certainly was not occurring through outdated policies of isolation. Indians needed, first, to be exposed to the cultural modernity of the core; once this happened, it was believed Indian's values and normative orientations would undergo a major transformation. In their very ethnocentric way, whites assumed that should Indians be given the choice, they would naturally accept the culture of whites over theirs; eventually, cultural integration would occur. This, however, did not happen.

Survival of traditional Indian nations, within a sea of modernity, is dependent on understanding essential differences of social organizations. For example, the social organization of the United States is often characterized by a wide division of labor, high level of urbanization, capital-intensive production, small nuclear family, bureaucratic structures, high per capita income, and norms and values that arise from such settings. On the other hand, traditional social organizations manifest a narrow division of labor, low or no level of urbanization, labor-intensive products, large extended family, lower per capita income, and traditional norms and values that often conflict with those of modern society.

Had economic integration occurred, it is highly probable Indian assimilation would have emulated that of immigrants. Economists suggest that as a group participates in the national economic system, changes in its social organizations occur and the group becomes more like the national character of the dominant society. However, this cultural integration did not occur to any large degree, for two reasons: one, the United States did not encourage it, but opted for increased dependency, possibly because it was less costly; and two, Indians did not desire integration; rather, they preferred separation.

It is thus fair to say that Indians realized early on that assimilation meant the eradication of their traditions and thus the eventual eradication of themselves. Their concern was highlighted by a major slogan: "kill the Indian. . . . save the man". Whites believed it was the *Indianness* of Indians that needed to be extinguished. However, Indians did not believe the two could be separated. Whites failed or refused to understand that initiatives that forced Indians onto small allotments of land and the demand that Indians acquire individual ownership of that land went against the core belief of Indians. To value individual rather than collective lifestyles was interpreted by Indians as an attempt to end their tribal identity and eventually them.

Religion, language, and land are the glues that bind people, and a collective ideology made up of a set of values and beliefs is the glue that binds a tribe. When a culture is tied so closely to land as it is in Native American culture, policies of integration have a monumental impact on that culture. Consequently, when certain traits of people are gone, culture has been essentially wiped out, and cultural genocide has occurred.

In the end, the United States failed to generate a policy that would successfully integrate Native Americans politically, socially, or economically. Since integration did not occur, government was in need of yet another policy that would facilitate assimilation. Therefore, from 1928 through 1945, several studies, reports, reforms, and Congressional responses developed on the Indian issue. As will be discussed in the following period, while very few of these policies did little to solve the "Indian problem" they did continue to have adverse effects on traditional Indian life and continued to chip away at any power traditional tribal governments may have been able to protract.

SELF-CONTROL: SELF-GOVERNMENT

With the election of Franklin D. Roosevelt and the inception of the New Deal came new legislation that addressed the Indian issue and sought reforms. The Meriam Report of 1928 was one of the first reports that thoroughly documented the plight of Indians. The report stated that the poverty of Indians and the failure of Indians to assimilate produced horrendous conditions. In response to these conditions, the investigation called for the creation of "increased appropriations to improve the diet of children in boarding schools, the creation of new positions in the fields of health and education, the construction of more Indian day schools, the repair of Indian Service buildings," and much more (Deloria and Lytle 1983, 44). Policy makers believed that an Indian government modeled after the U.S. government was the best. In other words, create an Indian government that was self-governing similar to the United States and improve the Indian–white relationship.

In order to create the conditions for a new era of Indian policymaking, John Collier, an avowed advocate of Indian rights, was appointed Commissioner of Indian Affairs by the Roosevelt Administration. Although Collier's major goal, like that of his predecessors, was assimilation, his tactics were slightly different in that he sought the active cooperation of Indians. Unfortunately, his ideas were shaped by his experiences with the tightly organized Pueblo people. Neither his background nor the background of many Indian reformers prepared them for the diversity of Indian interests and preferences. Collier, like so many before him, believed one stroke of the legislative pen could meet the interests of all tribes.

True to form, Congress obliged Collier by implementing the Indian Reorganization Act (IRA) in 1934, one hundred years after the first IRA, the Indian Removal Act. The major thrust behind the IRA was to divert power onto reservation governments and away from the federal government. The federal government believed that reorganized formal tribal governments should bear the responsibility of governing. Tribes would have to vote to accept or reject the provisions of the IRA. During the two-year period set as a deadline for tribes to vote, 258 elections were held. One hundred and eighty one tribes voted to accept the IRA provisions. The remaining 77 tribes rejected it, including the large Navajo tribe of 45,000 people.

Those tribes that accepted the IRA were then responsible for creating a tribal government that was supposed to be the mirror image of the federal government, thus making it easier for the federal government to administer its policies, and have a more government-to-government relationship. The act stripped the state of any jurisdiction on Indian land; ended the earlier allotment policy, stating "no land of any Indian reservation shall be allotted in severalty to any Indian" (Wax and Buchanan 1975, 37), and made it easier for the federal

47

government to allocate the necessary funds that many of these nations needed to survive by providing a revolving credit fund. However, similar to the GAA, this act continued to give the Secretary of the Interior increased power. The Secretary had the power to make loans to tribes if Indians pursued the Secretary's narrow definition of economic development.

Subsequently, Indian tribes experienced an array of responses to the implementation of the IRA. For some tribes, attempts to organize under the IRA brought disruption and heightened intratribal factional disputes. For others, it brought a much-needed organization, a revival or establishment of tribal government, tribal courts, police, and an improved economic position. Yet, while some tribes believed the IRA would help Indians self-governing, other tribes viewed the IRA as just another tool used by whites to impose their form of governing onto tribes. Other Indians viewed the IRA as giving a few federally appointed Indians dictatorial power, and thus created the conditions for the development of corrupt leadership.

Eventually, most tribes were administered IRA regulations regardless of how they voted. Indian nations would have to design a constitution, elect representatives, disentangle religion and politics, and bring about a new philosophy toward tribal rights and lands. This would erode traditional tribal governments and facilitate cultural transformation.

How ironic that a system so similar to the Iroquois Confederation, discussed in Chapter 2, would eventually be forced upon the very population whose ancestors created it several hundred years earlier. Naturally, this raises the question as to the purpose of politics in traditional and American societies. European ideologies suggest that as societies evolve, people are not capable of sustaining a level of free state as noted in the state of nature. Government thus becomes a necessary evil in order to control men's passions. If this is the case, the Iroquois society had progressed into an interesting combination of a society bearing all the traits of a free state and a developed government. Yet, because of U.S. imperialism and colonization, Indian societies were not at liberty to create tribal government founded on the ideals of the Iroquois Confederacy. Indigenous societies in the "New World" had a level of democracy not then realized in any part of the Old World. Paradoxically, by emulating the Iroquois Confederation, the U.S. Constitution provided the mechanism for political leaders to force a population to conform to the Europeans' standard of democracy.

THE OBJECTIVES OF THE IRA
1) Officially ended the policy of allotment.
2) Set up a revolving fund for purposes of economic development.
3) Tribes now had the right to organize for its common welfare, and adopt an appropriate constitution and bylaws (Getches et al 1993, 218–219).

Of all federal Indian legislation, the IRA is the most ambiguous in terms of effectiveness. While it did end the irrefutably egregious allotment period, in its own way it may have set the stage for the next policy to raise its ugly head.

FORCED ASSIMILATION: TERMINATION

After winning the presidency in 1952, the Republicans began a reversal of Roosevelt's programs and attempted to "free" the tribes of their colonial master (Wax and Buchanan 1975). In other words, massive cuts were initiated in Indian federal programs for health, education, and housing, referred to as "withdrawal programming." Funding for the previous Indian reorganizational period was attacked as well.

In June of 1953, Representative William Henry Harrison of Wyoming introduced House Concurrent Resolution 108. This Resolution stated that all Indian tribes located within the States of California, Florida, New York, and Texas should be freed from federal supervision and control, and all federal assistance discontinued. The Resolution was accepted and the federal government began cutting the dependency that was historically created within those designated states.

In August of 1953, Congress passed Public Law 280 (67 Stat. 588) known to Indians as termination. This law gave certain states jurisdiction over civil and criminal activities on many Indian reservations and limited tribal jurisdiction. Even though the system of tribal government was still an important part of negotiations that transpired between the United States and Indians, Public Law 280 significantly diminished tribal authority.

Arthur V. Watkins, a leading congressional proponent of termination, was firmly convinced—out of good faith and ignorance—that if the Indians were set free, they would soon become "productive citizens." He also believed that through termination the people of America would begin to treat Indians not as Indians but as fellow American citizens with no special treatments. The implementation of the Indian Citizenship Act of 1924 and the dissolution of tribes through termination would make this all possible.

Watkins' article entitled "Termination of Federal Supervision: The Removal of Restrictions over Indian Property and Person," written in 1932 (several years before Resolution 108 was proposed), adequately depicts termination as the best choice for Congress and the general public in dealing with the "Indian problem." This new choice by Congress, however, delivered much confusion, in some instances disasters, and in most cases provided a decade of controversy and facilitated Indian protests (Gates 1979, 47–49).

PUBLIC LAW 280

"Whereas it is the policy of Congress, as rapidly as possible to make the Indians within the territorial limits of the United States subject to the same laws and entitled to the same privileges and responsibilities as are applicable to other citizens of the United States, and to grant them all the rights and prerogatives pertaining to American citizenship; and whereas the Indians within the territorial limits of the United States should assume their full responsibilities as American citizens: Now therefore be it. . . (Getches et al 1993, 231).

From the very beginning of the Termination period, there were a number of non-Indians who opposed termination. Many Americans viewed termination as a method of robbing the Indians of the few services rightly deserved . Others believed that slow integration into larger society should continue until Indians themselves decide to terminate federal assistance. Many Indians viewed termination as the last effort to eliminate their Indian identity.

The controversy that mounted during this period was the main reason for the eventual demise of Resolution 108. Many white liberals and Indian Nationalists branded the termination policy as a great evil. States were not happy with the increased responsibility of assisting Indians, as this new policy would shift guardianship of Indians from the federal government on to states with fewer resources.

The support of opponents to forced termination was overwhelming. Many articles in the press encouraged Congress to review the possible consequences of termination. The public response apparently worked. Less than a decade later, in 1958, Secretary of the Interior Fred Steton announced that no tribe would be terminated without its consent.

Much like the Indian Reorganization Act, tribes could vote to be terminated. When tribes were terminated, tribal assets were liquidated and distributed to tribal members. In their article "The Evolution of the Termination Policy" (1977), Charles Wilkinson and Eric Biggs discuss the basic consequences of termination:

1) There were fundamental changes in landownership patterns.
2) The trust relationship between government and Indians ended.
3) State legislative jurisdiction was imposed.
4) State judicial authority was imposed.
5) Exemption from State taxing power was ended.
6) Special federal programs to tribes were discontinued.
7) Special federal programs to individual Indians were discontinued.
8) Tribal sovereignty was effectively ended.

However, it was not until President Nixon entered the White House that the fears of termination were alleviated completely. On July 8, 1970, President Nixon delivered a speech confronting the errors of termination:

> Because termination is morally and legally unacceptable, because it produces bad practical results, and because the mere threat of termination tends to discourage greater self-sufficiency among Indian groups, I'm asking the Congress to pass a new Concurrent Resolution which would expressly renounce, repudiate and repeal the termination policy as expressed in House Concurrent Resolution 108 of the 83rd Congress (Forbes 1981, 37).

Two tribes, the Menominee of Wisconsin and the Klamath of Oregon, among the twelve that were terminated eventually, were restored as federally recognized tribes; the Menominee in 1973 and the Klamath in 1986. Restoration of federal status did not happen, however, without grass-roots organization of both tribes.

At best, this policy was an invention of a few aggressive politicians wishing to hastily incorporate the dependent group into the core. This no doubt was the reason for extending citizenship to Indians in 1924, and of the reorganization period. Both of these policies were intended to transform Indians, but they did not work in the manner expected. What these two policies did do, however, was to open the door to the possibility of termination. The federal government could not terminate a population of a distinct and different national identity without ensuring its incorporation into the American national identity. The passage of the Indian Citizenship Act in 1924 assisted the incorporation of Indians into larger society. The IRA began transforming the institutions and structures of tribal governments. Naturally, Termination became easier to apply with the passage of these two bills, at least in theory.

Still for Indians, an unexpected positive aspect of the termination proposal surfaced. The very idea of ending tribal governments and ending the national identity of Indians galvanized Native activism. This policy provided an opportunity for Native insurgency to develop, an insurgency that was in its incubation period for many years. Politicians soon realized that the very idea of termination was a politically explosive issue. This in turn forced politicians to return to the drawing board and develop a new Indian policy that had the potential of suppressing Native activists and their supporters during the early years of the 1960s.

NEOCOLONIALISM: SELF-DETERMINATION

From 1960 to the 1980s, a different approach to the formation of policies regarding Indians was developed. While the termination period seemed to have destroyed a portion of Indian culture and encroached substantially upon the attempts of Indians to remain Indian, Indians were able to see some slight improvements in education and health services and gain increased control of their destiny.

After the assassination of President Kennedy, President Johnson proposed "a new goal for our Indian programs; a goal that ended the old debate about termination and stressed self-determination" (Levitan and Hetrick 1971, 195). These programs emphasized a greater need to wipe out a defined portion of the American population known as "the poor." Public assistance would play an increasingly important role in the lives of poor people during this period and an even larger part for Indians.

President Johnson's War on Poverty made it possible to create legislation where tribes could apply some semblance of self-determination. The Area Redevelopment Administration Act is one example of the type of acts that permeated the minds of the executive branch in the early 1960s. This act stressed the importance of allowing Indians a chance to develop their resources while still not severing their tie to the federal government. Another act, the Economic Opportunity Act (EOA), passed in 1964, provided Indians with a form of self-determination through community organizing. The EOA, an antipoverty program, stressed the importance of allowing Indians to create and implement community activities with minimal interference from federal agencies. Although many reservations are badly in need of housing, education, health services, economic development, and manpower assistance, the mere presence of the Indian Community Action Program (a branch of the EOA) indicates the desire for tribal councils to adopt resolutions that curtail federal supervision and allow tribes to produce constructive projects to eradicate the poverty most Indian nations were experiencing.

ERA OF SELF-DETERMINATION (1961—Present)

"The principal legislative initiative to emerge from the Nixon proposals, the Indian Self-Determination and Education Assistance Act of 1975, gives express authority to the Secretaries of Interior and Health and Human Services to contract with, and make grants to, Indian tribes and other Indian organizations for the delivery of federal services. The Act reflects a fundamental philosophical change concerning the administration of Indian affairs; tribal programs are funded by the federal government, but the programs should be planned and administered by the tribes themselves; federal "domination" should end" (Getches et al 1993, 255).

During the self-determination period, the following three pieces of legislation stand out as portraying change in policies set forth by the federal government: (Deloria and Lytle, 1983).

> 1) The Indian Education Act of 1972 provided special training programs for teaching Indian children, and provided a base for including Indian participation.

> 2) The Indian Self-Determination and Education Assistance Act of 1975: Directed the Secretary of the Interior to confer with the tribe to plan, conduct, and administer programs. In other words, the act permitted the tribe, not the BIA or any other branch of federal government, to decide if Indians wished to participate in any given program.

> 3) American Indian Policy Review Commission of 1974: Authorized two-year commission to review existing federal policies and make recommendations for position change.

The passing of these three pieces of legislation seemed to have increased the need for more federal bureaucratic involvement. Realizing federal involvement was still part of Indian life, proponents of self-determination were willing to accept the intrusion, but only temporarily. Many tribal members believe that until certain institutions are created and until tribes gain the capabilities needed for self-governing, the impact of sudden "freedom" could be disastrous for Indian nations. They suggest that efforts to provide more viable institutions and a greater ability among Indians to exercise their independence must be combined with a gradual expansion of self-determination.

What benefits Indians experienced came at an enormous price. In order to receive any of the funds generated through national social welfare legislation, Indians often had to pose as a racial minority, even though there were major differences in the grievances and demands of Indians and those of domestic minorities. The self-determination of Indians could not be met by integrationist policies or through piecemeal reforms created for minorities. Therefore, while these types of reforms seemed to have appeased national minorities, they galvanized Indian activism. Indians realized that with the implementation of these types of policies came a loss of a culture, an increase in U.S. bureaucratic involvement, and a decrease in true self-determination.

The federal government passed numerous amendments and statutes to bring about assimilation and cultural transformation. Historically, two major ones stand out: the Act of July 31, 1882, and the Indian Citizenship Act. The Act of July 31, 1882, designated army posts and barracks as places to train "nomadic tribes having educational treaty claims upon the United States" (Deloria and Lytle 1983, 11). The act was the beginning of a commitment on the part of the federal government to educate Indians while really focusing on Christianizing, civilizing, and instilling ideas of capital liberalism. The Citizenship Act assumed that by giving citizenship (to the only people in the United States who did not desire it) Indians would naturally adopt American values and assimilate. The main thrust of both of these acts failed. Assimilation or cultural transformation did not occur to any large degree. However, what did occur can be linked to Indian activism and not to any one policy.

There were some legislative victories for Indians that were a result of the Indian activism. Following are five acts that many Indian activists worked to achieve:

1) The 1975 Indian Self-Determination and Educational Assistance Act allows tribes to manage their own housing, health, and other programs with less interference from the Secretary of the Interior.
2) The 1978 American Religious Freedom Act gives Indians freedom to practice their traditional religions on reservations.
3) The 1978 Indian Child Welfare Act gives tribal government authority over the child custody proceedings.
4) The 1990 Indian Arts and Crafts Act was passed to promote Native American artwork and business, reduce foreign and counterfeit product competition, and stop deceptive marketing practices.

5) The 1991 Native American Graves Protection and Repatriation Act established that Native American tribal groups own or control human remains or cultural items that are discovered on tribal and federal lands. In addition, these objects must be returned to tribes upon their request.

The Indian Child Welfare Act (ICWA) is seen as a major victory for Indian nations and individual Indians. The ICWA was designed to stop the wholesale removal of reservation children by state welfare agencies, state courts, and many religious individuals. The stated purpose of the ICWA is not only to protect the best interests of Indian children but also to protect Indian parents and Indian tribes. Until the passage of the ICWA, Congress discovered that approximately one-third of reservation Indian children had been removed from their families and placed in boarding schools, government homes, adoptive families, foster care, or other institutions often without the approval or consent of parents or tribes.

There is no doubt that the earlier federal Indian legislation and specific historical circumstances such as war, massacres, and U.S. economic development shaped contemporary tribal governments; these are discussed in the following chapter. To understand how the transformation of modern forms of tribal government developed, a comprehensive analysis of *tribalization* must be developed. Cornell (1988) defines *tribalization* as the process of how tribes have become what they are today. In other words, if we are to understand the next chapter that deals with modern forms of tribal governments, we must understand how the pre-stated various historical policies worked to chip away at tribal sovereignty until it looked more like the *politics of interference* by courts, Congress, the BIA, and, increasingly, state governments and corporations.

The policies, whether they were of removal, relocation, reorganization, or termination, were created to provide economic incentives and in the end promote assimilation, that is, stop Indians from being Indian and integrate into larger society. While none of these policies proved to be successful in fulfilling their intent, these policies did contribute to a different type of Indian. In the late 1960s, Indians began reacting to poor legislation in a very organized fashion. For the first time since the arrival of the Europeans, Indians demanded that Indian legislation be created and influenced by Indians. No doubt, this change in demands contributed to the five pieces of legislation noted above, but they also contributed to a very different tribal government, as discussed in the following chapter.

QUESTIONS FOR DISCUSSION:

1) What are the main tenets of the Doctrine of Discovery?

2) Explain how Christianization, civilization, and capitalism occurred with the acquisition of individual land.

3) What were the purposes and the consequences of Resolution 108?

4) In what ways does the self-determination period end domination of the federal government, or does it?

5) To what extent did the Indian Removal Act protect Indians?

CHAPTER FIVE

LEVELS OF TRIBAL SOVEREIGNTY

So long as a tribe exists and remains in possession of its lands, its title and possession are sovereign and exclusive; and there exists no authority to enter upon their lands, for any purpose whatever, without their consent (U. S. Attorney General Wirt, 1821 in Stuart 2005, 177).

The key to understanding how various nations function is to determine the forms by which they are governed. As stated previously, the method of how Indian nations are governed fluctuates according to the needs of larger American society rather than the needs of Indians. If land was needed, Indians were removed and relocated, if not annihilated. The Cherokee Nation case demonstrates this well. If Indian nations were determined to be uncivilized, the federal government passed the General Allotment Act (GAA) in hopes of not only civilizing them but also Christianizing them and creating the conditions for them to be part of the focus on economic development. Moreover, if Indian nations were found to be too traditional, too disorganized, or not functioning as their legal guardian stated they should, tribes were forced to reorganize under the Indian Reorganization Act (IRA), 1934.

Twenty-some years after this reorganization period, in the early 1950s, corporations began to eye resources that were not developed on the shrinking Indian land base. True to form, the federal government obliged corporate needs. Similar to the *Cherokee Nation* case, the federal government created a justification to remove Indians and give corporate access to the very land Indians historically resisted developing. This repetitive method of treatment demonstrates the various forms, on how Indian nations were governed: largely the politics of interference, as stated in the previous chapter. Therefore, it is fair to say that tribal governments are shaped by the actions of, and in reaction to, policies of the federal government. Simply put, levels of tribal sovereignty on any given Indian nation at any given time fluctuate according to the federal government.

As stated in Chapter 2, early Indigenous populations within the Western Hemisphere relied upon a variety of activities when negotiating with other tribes; that is to say, long before the Europeans arrived and forced the original inhabitants to change their methods of governing, Indigenous people were *politicking*. More importantly, these various Indian nations were sovereign powers long before Chief Justice Marshall defined them creatively as

Domestic Dependent Nations, as noted by Felix Cohen in the following paragraph:

> Indian sovereignty is the principle that those powers which are lawfully vested in an Indian tribe, are not, in general, delegated powers granted by express acts of congress, but rather inherent powers of a limited sovereignty which has never been extinguished. Each Indian tribe begins its relationship with the federal government as a sovereign power, recognized as such in treaty and legislation (Cohen1942).

Unfortunately, Anglo-American political and legal theory, practice, and perceptions do not provide any consistent interpretation of tribal sovereignty. Marshall invented the domestic dependent status, believing that tribes would eventually become states and the *withering away* of dependency would eventually follow. This *withering away* did not occur fast enough, so Congress offered termination in the 1950s. Similar to other policies, termination did not take hold, and hence the level of sovereignty continued to fluctuate somewhere between absolute and inherent sovereignty, or, as implied earlier, as sovereign as Congress allows tribes to be.

In essence, tribal governments have the same powers as the federal and state governments to regulate their internal affairs, with a few exceptions. Historically, Congress has placed a number of explicit limitations on a tribe's power to use or sell their land. Still, there are nine important areas of tribal authority. Tribes have the right to:

1) form a government.
2) determine tribal membership.
3) regulate tribal property.
4) regulate individual property.
5) tax.
6) maintain law and order.
7) exclude nonmembers from Indian territory.
8) regulate domestic relations.
9) regulate commerce and trade (Pevar 1992).

Many tribal governments desire *absolute* sovereignty, particularly when making decisions about culture, education, health, economic development, and most other matters regarding tribal affairs. In addition, even though the Supreme Court's affirmation of tribal sovereignty occurred significantly in the 1980s in a number of cases decided, by the end of the decade the high court was no longer voting on the side of tribal sovereignty. Moreover, Congress and other key actors began to fervently oppose tribal sovereignty, especially in decisions regarding gaming, fishing, water, and mineral rights. This suggests that what little sovereignty tribes had acquired was slowly eroding. The bureaucratic maze shows that any initiative started by Tribal Councils must go to the Bureau of Indian Affairs and up to the Secretary of the Interior, who rejects it or supports it.

There are numerous events and issues that have the capacity to determine and shape a tribe's level of sovereignty. First, which European power(s) (the French, Dutch, Spanish, English, or Russian), may have set different patterns of interactions? Second, what treaties were made and subsequently broken that may provide the tribe with litigation opportunities? Third, what was the experience of tribes with removal and relocation and various other federal Indian policies? Fourth, what was the level of interaction between culturally different tribes that were forced to share a land base? Fifth, within what state is the tribal government? Sixth, what types of resources are in the tribal nation? More importantly, what level of sovereignty do the various tribal governments desire: absolute sovereignty, shared sovereignty, or a form of self-governing?

Currently, the issue that determines tribal sovereignty more than any other is the development of natural resources on Indian Territory. If an Indian nation has resources desired by larger society or corporations, federal Indian legislation is often shaped by those interests rather than the interests of the tribe, regardless of other issues. Nations that have water, uranium, coal, natural gas, agriculture, or other resources often confront legislation that seeks to develop these resources. For example, individuals in the large Navajo Nation experienced relocation because Peabody Coal Company desired access to a large body of coal on the shared land of the Navajo and Hopi. Similarly, the Lummi Nation in Washington battled commercial and game fishers supported by state and federal governments to secure their fishing rights guaranteed in an 1855 treaty. Both of these nations have asserted tribal sovereignty in different ways that they may represent the interests of their members.

However, it was not until after the Boldt Decision in 1974 that the Lummi were able to reclaim some of their fishing rights. This right was achieved largely because of a strong tribal government and native protests opposing numerous state and federal actors, as well as a supportive judge. In the District Court for Washington, Judge George H. Boldt's decision held that Indian people possess an unequivocal right to fish at all "usual and unaccustomed places," whether on or off present reservations, and an equivalent right to participate in regional fisheries management. For his decision, Judge Boldt was the focus of protest and harassment that called for his impeachment by the Ku Klux Klan, the John Birch Society, several anti-Indian coalition groups, including state and local officials, local sporting organizations, and commercial fishing industry. This incident demonstrates what tribes and some judges are prepared to do to secure treaty rights.

Unfortunately, the large Navajo Nation was not so successful. The Navajo Tribal Council began approving mineral extraction with large corporations as early as 1952. Their actions were not unusual. In their efforts to provide jobs and stimulate their economies, various tribal governments often enter into agreements with corporations, only to regret it later. Unlike Indians, once corporations are on Indian land, it is very difficult to get them relocated. Moreover, when examining the 1974 Navajo-Hopi Settlement Act, the purpose and consequences were not all that different than the 1830 Indian Relocation Act. Under the guise of "protectionism," the federal government removed Indians. A basic difference was the arrival of new actors, corporations. Peabody Coal Company desired access to the coal, and the federal government gave them access by removing Indians.

Since the creation of the IRA, and because tribal governments created court systems, Congress often defers to these courts to establish laws and codes in regulating many aspects of the tribe. There are instances, however, when there is no clear distinction as to which court or which agency has power within Indian country, particularly when it comes to freedoms and rights. As noted in the following subcommittee hearing in 1977, the subject of Indian rights is complex and ambiguous:

> It is almost always a mistake to seek answers to Indian legal issues by making analogies to seemingly similar fields. General notions of civil rights law and public land laws, for example, simply fail to resolve many questions relating to American Indian tribes and individuals. This extraordinary body of law and policy holds its own answers, which are often wholly unexpected to those unfamiliar with it (Pevar 1992, Introduction).

For example, we can see how ambiguous Indian rights are when examining religious rights. "Congress shall make no law respecting an establishment of religion, or prohibiting the free exercise thereof. . . ." The First Amendment, adopted in 1791, supports the claim that the United States was founded on religious freedoms. In reality, America was originally founded on the right to own property and religious freedom of Protestants, later to include other religions. It was not until 1978 that Congress took positive steps to guarantee Native Americans the same religious freedoms as other Americans. The American Indian Religion Act reads:

> Henceforth it shall be the policy of the United States to protect and preserve for American Indians their inherent rights of freedom to believe, express, and exercise the traditional religions of the Americans, Eskimo, Aleut, and Native Hawaiians, including but not limited to access to sites, use and possession of sacred objects, and the freedom to worship through ceremonies and traditional rites (Petoskey 1985, 233).

Obviously, the religious practices of American Indians on tribal land were not protected by the First Amendment, and therefore required special legislation. Since many of the standards for Indian legislation have been based on Judeo-Christian religions, many of them, like the one above, cannot be fully implemented or accommodated without some level of conflict. In order for Indians to practice their religion, they often require access to a pristine environment or in some cases the use of a substance deemed illegal by states or federal government. Tribes argue their religious rights are violated when the federal land they use to practice their beliefs face economic development. Consequently, government must violate the religious rights of Indians in its pursuit of economic interests, suggesting economic interests virtually override Indian religious rights. The issue of Indian rights to religious expression is denied when the expression of religious rights conflict with the economic rights of Americans, as stated in Chapter 3 with the Lyng case of 1988.

Many theorists support Max Weber's (1904) notion that no other religion facilitates capitalism quite like Protestantism. While it is difficult to dispute or support this notion, it can be stated with certainty that many of the beliefs of Indians run counter to U.S. economic development. Had Indians become Christians, as many of them are today, it is highly unlikely there would have been a need for much of the cultural transformation legislation directed at making them Christians. Early Americans believed that if one was a Christian, they were automatically civilized and would thus develop the land God had sent them to develop. This is partially why Indians needed their own religious freedom act. Yet, as can be seen in the opinion of Justice Sandra Day O'Connor, U.S. economic interests outweigh Indian religious rights. More than likely, U.S. economic interests outweigh all religious rights. However, no other religion in the United States challenges the rights to economically develop land as those of land-based religions.

Another act that interferes extensively with the rights of tribes is the Major Crimes Act of 1885. In passing this Act, the federal government spread its jurisdictional wings over Indian country. At the time of passing this Act, the federal government had jurisdiction over seven crimes: murder, manslaughter, rape, assault with intent to kill, arson, burglary, and larceny. Today, it has increased its jurisdiction to include additional crimes. Nonetheless, the problem has little to do with jurisdiction and more to do with the lack of sufficient law enforcement resources. The FBI, which investigates federal crimes, often gives reservation crime a low priority. Consequently, with conviction rates low, violent crimes on Indian reservations escalate. Rather than give tribal government any jurisdiction, the federal government lets numerous crimes go uninvestigated and numerous criminals not held accountable.

States may not exercise authority over tribes unless specifically authorized by Congress or by the tribes, but they too have historically tried to assert their power within native territory. This intrusion by the federal government and states leaves tribal governments with limited jurisdiction. Moreover, even though tribal governments are recognized as having a higher status than that of states, they nonetheless continue to be subordinate to and dependent on the U.S. federal government in ways that states are not.

One area where the federal government has allowed tribes to assert themselves is in determining their tribal membership. Tribes define their membership by emphasizing descendants, meaning anyone descended from Indians, by residency, or blood quantum. On the one hand, the federal government defines an American Indian as someone having one-fourth Indian blood and enrolled in a federally recognized tribe. On the other hand, many tribes require members to have anywhere from one-eighth to one-half tribal blood. The so-called "blood quantum" policies became an implicit part of federal Indian legislation beginning in 1887 as part of the GAA, as noted in Chapter 4. Congress had hoped that by setting a degree of Indian blood standard, Indians would intermarry or assimilate and eventually be defined out of existence. While this has not occurred, the "blood quantum" of one-fourth is the current federal standard to determine who is Indian, particularly when deciding who receives federal assistance

Today, the purpose or function of having a "blood quantum," a "Certificate of Degree of Indian Blood," or any method of deciding who is Indian is seen by many Indians as just another attempt of the classic "divide and conquer" strategy: pitting Indians against Indians and/or Indians against those individuals that do not have "enough" Indian blood. In some cases, whenever the question of someone's *Indianness* is raised, it is usually about who will receive the few federal crumbs the BIA or the Secretary of the Interior is tossing at individual Indians. How Indians themselves determine who is Indian has less to do with the level of Indian blood and more to do with the extent to which that person is working collectively to increase tribal sovereignty and other Indian rights. To adopt the identity without adopting the struggle contributes nothing to the expansion of tribal sovereignty, suggest many Indian activists.

In the following case, the Supreme Court sided with tribal sovereignty. This case demonstrates that the federal government is often eager to support tribal sovereignty as long as it does not interfere with the rights, usually defined as economic rights, of Americans. This particular case is also explained in Chapter 8.

MARTINEZ V. SANTA CLARA PUEBLO NATION

Martinez, a member of the Santa Clara Pueblo Nation, brought a suit against her tribe because it did not recognize her daughter as a member. Santa Clara Pueblos consider children of male tribal members eligible for membership, but children of female members who marry nonmembers, as Ms. Martinez did, were viewed as ineligible. The Santa Clara Pueblo is a patriarchal society where membership is defined through the father. The Supreme Court agreed with the tribe's argument that tribal membership is a matter for the tribe to determine, not the federal government. Consequently, the child of Ms. Martinez cannot be tribally enrolled in either tribe even though she is a full-blooded Indian.

However, in the following 1978 case, government went against tribal sovereignty by stating tribes could not make any laws that violated their members' right to religious freedom even though the federal government had historically denied Indians this right. In 1880, in an attempt to Christianize Indians, the federal government prohibited the practice of many traditional ceremonies, specifically the Ghost Dance. Indian agents greatly feared the Ghost Dance movement because it inspired the Lakota to believe that by practicing this dance the white man would leave Indian land. After years of being denied religious freedom, the American Indian Religious Freedom Act was passed in 1978.

> **NATIVE AMERICAN CHURCH V. NAVAJO TRIBAL COUNCIL**
> In 1958, the Navajo Tribal Council enacted an ordinance making it illegal to bring peyote onto the Navajo reservation and thus restricted the use of Navajo members of the Native American Church to use peyote in their ceremonies. The Native American Church filed a suit against the tribe in federal court. In 1994, Congress passed an amendment to the American Indian Religious Freedom Act of 1978 guaranteeing the rights of Native Americans to possess, transport, and use peyote in the course of traditional religious ceremonies.

As can be seen in the previous three cases, the level of tribal sovereignty fluctuates according to the issue. In the Lyng case, sovereignty was denied because it interfered with U.S. economic rights. In the Martinez case, tribal sovereignty was supported because it had to do with tribal membership. With the peyote case, the Navajo Tribal Council was denied sovereignty because this case dealt with a tribal council asserting its sovereignty by denying its members religious freedom. In all three of these cases, as in all American Indian cases, the Supreme Court made the ruling.

There is a more recent case that illustrates confusion regarding a tribe's level of sovereignty. As mentioned earlier, tribal governments have the right to determine their citizens by using an assortment of factors that emphasize descendants, residency, or blood quantum. For example, some tribes use the blood-quantum mechanism most typically used by the federal government to assign identification, but increase it from one-fourth to one-half or lower it to one-sixteenth. In most cases, as demonstrated in the Martinez case above, the Supreme Court allows tribes to determine membership. However, the recent case of the Cherokee Freedmen is very interesting and currently has not gone before the Supreme Court, and it might not. For now, this case is playing itself out in the court of public opinion and in Congress.

In 2007, a Cherokee Nation Constitutional amendment was voted on that required that the nation's citizens have at least one Indian ancestor on the Dawes Rolls, the primary document used to determine Cherokee Nation eligibility. The reason for the amendment was to qualify who was Cherokee and who could live in the Cherokee Nation. There were some individuals defined as "freedmen" who the Cherokee people believed did not qualify for membership. In the early 1800s, some Cherokees acquired slaves. These slaves accompanied the Cherokee on the "Trail of Tears", during forced removal. By 1861, there were 4,000 black slaves living among the Cherokee. After the Civil War, the tribe signed a treaty that granted former slaves, or freemen, all the rights of the Native Cherokee. By 2007, the Cherokee amended their constitution, making "Indian blood" a requirement for Cherokee citizenship. Subsequently, some 2,800 descendants of Cherokee freedmen would be excluded from citizenship; they were told to leave the reservation. The treaty between the Cherokee Nation and the United States in 1866 stated that the free colored persons who were on Cherokee land are now residents of the Cherokee Nation and shall have all the rights of Native Cherokees.

The Cherokee Nation states that if they had the sovereignty to decide Freedmen could be enrolled in 1866, they now had the sovereignty to dis-enroll them in 2007. This case went before the Cherokee Supreme Court, and the court stated that they could not overturn the will of the people.

What is interesting about this case is that the Freedmen appealed to the Black Caucus, representatives of Congress who represent the interests of African Americans. The Black Caucus along with other congressional members threatened to stop all federal funding to the Cherokee Nation if the Nation did not re-enroll the Freedmen. At this time, the Cherokee Nation is sticking with its decision to dis-enroll 2,800 freedmen and other non-Indians whose descendants are not on the Dawes Roll. In the summer of 2012, the federal government filed a countersuit against the Cherokee Nation to determine Freedmen descendants' eligibility for tribal citizenship. In this suit, the federal government is requesting a decision that would allow the Freedmen to retain their citizenship rights and prohibit the Cherokee Nation from dis-enrolling them. In February of 2014, President Obama sided with the freedmen to stay as Cherokee members.

This case demonstrates the fragility of tribal sovereignty as numerous actors with various interests and power involve themselves into a key power given to tribal governments. Unfortunately, there is no American Indian Caucus that could represent the interests of Indians in the same way the Black Caucus represents the Freedmen. There would have been a more equal balance of power between Indians and the Freedmen if there had been an American Indian Caucus. This case illustrates the limited power of tribes when it comes to a key part of self-determination, citizenship.

LAW ENFORCEMENT

Because there are approximately 2.1 million Indians belonging to 511 culturally distinct federally recognized tribes, it is unrealistic to expect tribal governments to create and enforce the same laws in a similar fashion. Some tribes have very strong and effective courts, and others do not. Indian nations have the inherent right to exercise civil jurisdiction but not criminal jurisdiction. Usually, tribes have jurisdiction over tribal members regarding such issues as marriage, divorce, and an assortment of other issues as long as they comply with tribal law. Obviously, tribal courts have jurisdiction only within the territory of their nation and not beyond their defined territory. However, whether the nation has total, concurrent, or shared jurisdiction with state and federal government will be largely determined by the crime, the location, and the identity of the victim and the accused.

If the crime is a misdemeanor and involves non-Indians, the state normally has jurisdiction. In a misdemeanor that involves an Indian and non-Indian, jurisdiction belongs to the federal government. Tribal courts have some jurisdiction when a misdemeanor and major crime involve Indians. While this method is most often used to determine jurisdiction, the question of what court has jurisdiction depends on the whims of federal and state interests. It is only when two Indians are involved in a crime that the tribe could have total jurisdiction, particularly if the crime is minor. Complications arise when the individuals are from different tribal nations. When this occurs, tribal governments must agree on the sentence. In many cases, it is not unheard of for tribal courts to ask offenders to pay compensation to the victim or to the victim's community. Some tribes continue to punish some crimes by a ritualistic whipping, or by banishing the guilty individual.

The following table identifies who has jurisdiction when a "major" crime is committed. It can be confusing, to say the least. However, what is all the more problematic is when the federal government has proven to be very incompetent in handling its responsibility to prosecute crimes on reservations. Jurisdiction is one thing, prosecution is quite another.

MAJOR CRIMES	
Persons Involved	*Jurisdiction*
—Indian accused Indian victim	Federal government (MCA)
—Indian accused non-Indian victim	Federal government
—Non-Indian accused Indian victim	Federal government
NONMAJOR CRIMES	
—Indian accused Indian victim	Tribal government
—non-Indian accused Indian victim	Federal government
—Indian accused non-Indian victim	Federal Government
—Indian accused, Indian victim	Tribal Government

(Pevar 1992, 132)

Obviously, tribal governments that are strong and have the capital to pursue the interest of the tribe are the most successful in asserting and guaranteeing self-government. Similar to states, tribal governments exercise power regarding taxation, economic regulations, zoning, extradition, the regulation of domestic and family relations, health care, housing, education, and much more. However, this power is frequently constrained, changed, and even extinguished by the actions of the federal government (as shown in the Freedmen case above) and states, particularly if tribal decisions should infringe on the rights of larger society.

For the past one hundred plus years, the federal government dominated tribal governments, this is well demonstrated in Chapter 4. However, in the last thirty years, tribal governments have been asserting their sovereignty by lobbying Congress, negotiating with state governments, and making demands mainly through the courts. Naturally, a major obstacle of tribes in representing the interests of their members is the poor structures of government, some of which were created during the reorganizational period in the 1930s. However, sovereignty has a greater potential to increase as these structures improve and as tribes increase their negotiating skills; we have seen this occur with the arrival of gaming in Indian country.

Gambling is a part of many traditional Indian cultures, but it was not eyed with any seriousness as a form of generating economic profits until the late 1970s and early 1980s. Several tribes, especially in California and Florida, opened up bingo parlors to earn revenue. In response to the cuts in federal funding to Indian Nations imposed during the Reagan Administration, tribes began eyeing the building of casinos. Today, revenues generated in these establishments can be substantial. The National Indian Gaming Association states that as of 2004, 12% of Indian gaming establishments generate 65% of Indian revenues. Therefore, gaming has the potential of assisting a small number of tribes that face high rates of poverty, unemployment, school dropout, and other indicators of poverty and social distress.

Gaming is a topic that continues to be hotly debated. Many members continue to vote against this form of economic development. Tribal members against gaming suggest that tribal governments that incorporate Anglo-American values are faulty because they cannot and do not adequately protect Indian cultural values. In most cases, tribal members suggest American values work against traditional cultural values. No doubt, Indian values such as consensus versus majority rule, community rather than individualism, and a holistic approach to religion and politics are compromised to the point of extinction within some contemporary tribal governments. This raises the question as to the extent to which tribal governments can be efficient and traditional at the same time or whether they must give up their traditional values in order to interact on a government-to- government relationship. Naturally, having all tribal governments structured the same and with the same values as American society would make it easier for the federal government to administer policies that reflect the needs of larger society. That is to say, if tribes held the same values as larger society, there would be little for government to act as a trustee or a guardian and thus the end of federal Indian legislation. Indians would comply, conform, and participate with the U.S. Government, with no need for federal Indian legislation. If there were no differences and no tribal status, Indians would be legally defined as an ethnic group, and their strategies for self-interest would be very similar to those of dominant minorities.

We know that is not about to happen. However, we do know that as governments of all types become stronger, there is little doubt they are better equipped to shape their governments in ways that support the interests of their members, whether they are traditional, modern, or a mixture of the two. More importantly, the level of sovereignty exercised by tribal governments will continue to be highly dependent upon two factors: the federal government recognizing and treating them as sovereign, and the tactical responses of tribal governments to the various actors. It is within this context that tribal governments are increasingly becoming political actors and edging toward a higher level of sovereignty. The next chapter discusses the sustainability of tribal identity and how who is Indian can have major consequences not only on who is a citizen of a Native Nation, but also on tribal sovereignty.

QUESTIONS FOR DISCUSSION:

1) Why is it important to define Indian Nations as Domestic Dependent Nations?

2) What was the impetus for the Indian Religious Rights Act? What does the Lyng Case illustrate?

3) If an Indian should kill a non-Indian on an Indian Nation other than their nation, who has jurisdiction?

4) Why is tribal sovereignty in its application so complex, ambiguous, and fictitious?

5) How should the Freedmen case be decided and handled?

CHAPTER SIX

Reclaiming and Sustaining a Tribal Cultural Identity

Set the blood quantum at one-quarter, hold to it as a rigid definition of Indians, let intermarriage proceed as it had for centuries, and eventually Indians will be defined out of existence. When that happens, the federal government will be freed of its persistent "Indian problem." (Limmerick 1987, 338).

Among the various issues facing American Indians today, one of the most controversial and hotly debated is that of Indian identity. The federal government created numerous pieces of legislation to first destroy the indigenous tribal identity and then set in motion a series of situations, events, and policies that would invent a new Indian identity, one that would more aptly fit the needs of Euro-Americans. This new identity is by all accounts a political identity, lacking any relationship to tribal nationalism, religion, class, culture, language, history, or traditions. Previous chapters traced the steps taken by government to repress the indigenous identity and addressed some of the tactics used by Indians to reclaim it. However, exploring and reclaiming any of the numerous heritages within the United States is difficult enough, but to reclaim a heritage that has historically been defined as savage, pagan, uncivilized, and un-American, makes the process all the more formidable. The yearning to find a tribal identity leads many people to join a community of Indians involved in traditional ceremonies, activities, and practices. Participating in such activities as powwows, sweat lodges, vision quests, and learning from elders about the daily rhythms of native life can facilitate the creation of a lost Indian identity, or, as Elizabeth Cook-Lynn so cleverly wrote in *Why I can't read Wallace Stegner and other Essays,* 1996, learning to commemorate Thanksgiving from a different side of the table.

The following interviews illustrate a common theme with which many contemporary Indians wrestle in search of a native identity (Watson and Meranto 2001).

> Mark describes his awakening to his Indian heritage in the following way: "My father was Taos, my mother of Mexican descent. Yet because of anti-Indian prejudices in the Denver community, my father shielded me and my siblings by raising us as Hispanics and not educating us to his Indian heritage." Mark said that he almost became an apple, red on the outside and white on the inside. It was only in young adulthood that his father began to share with his children

their rich Native heritage. "We are learning who we are, what we are, and what we can become with our Native ways and we are attempting to reintegrate our Native ways into our day-to-day lives." Mark has integrated some Indian ceremonies into his life in an effort to understand his heritage.

Dawnyel was adopted as a baby by a nonnative couple and raised in a culture closely resembling that of Chicano culture. She describes her household as a loving one, with hardworking and attentive parents. Of her Lakota Indian heritage, she says, "I was a victim of the American Holocaust, but nonetheless a survivor. It means that it is my job as a Native to educate others about the injustice and political agendas against my people. It means that I have inherited the love for Mother Earth that my ancestors possessed and struggled and suffered for. I am proud and would prefer to be none other than Indian." Dawnyel is learning to dance and hopes to participate in a powwow soon.

Marie, a Roman Catholic nun, describes herself as Native woman/Franciscan sister. She was born in Lakota territory and attended Indian boarding schools for twelve years. Her father spoke Lakota. He was a very gifted man intellectually and socially. He was also a lifetime alcoholic, unable to deal with ordinary family issues. "My mother was an extraordinary woman who managed to blend a victim mentality with pleasant survival techniques. She loved us despite these two sides of her personality." Marie shared the conflict she has felt between the two worlds of Native woman and Franciscan sister. She has reconciled these worlds "by attempting to have within me the spiritual memory of my Lakota ancestors who seek a voice through me." She keeps uppermost in her mind and her work the four Lakota values: wisdom, generosity, courage, and humility.

Zia was removed from her Navajo mother at the age of four and placed in an Indian government home. After running away from the home, she was subsequently placed in three different foster homes, all of which were white Christian fundamentalists. She did not learn she was Navajo until she was 21, when she finally met her mother. Her understanding of her Indian-ness has evolved as a result of becoming an activist and an academic. She loves attending powwows because for three days she is not viewed as a minority. She can absorb, observe, and not be judged. "Powwows are part recreational, ceremonial and spiritual for me. I don't feel compelled to conform to any specific kind of authenticity or to a set of stereotypes of who is Indian," she said.

While the American Indians above come from different life-experiences, they share a common desire to reclaim their Indian-ness and keep their cultural identity alive. Many of them look to various activities as an effective vehicle to attain, reclaim, and sustain their Indian identity. Through its various activities, the powwow, for example, supports the concept that discovering or creating an identity cannot be done in isolation. As political philosopher Charles Taylor noted, "an identity is created through a collective, through dialogue, partly overt, partly internal, with others" (1992, 34). An Indian activity brings individual Indians together, and creates a *we* out of the numerous Indian experiences. This process enables Indians to remain separate, if desired, while encouraging them to recognize and respect others' differences, whether these differences developed out of forced experiences or grew out of the evolutionary process that all cultures experience.

DESTROYING NATIVE CULTURE

In an effort to solve the "Indian problem," the federal government embraced Lieutenant Richard Pratt's motto, *kill the Indian and save the man.* U.S. policy makers believed Indian characteristics were an impediment to economic development and must be changed. Pratt suggested the only way to transform Indians was to remove them from their tribal environment, place them with white families and educate them. In 1879, Pratt convinced government that with federal funds he could socialize Indian children to accept a new set of norms, values, and ideas that, at the very least, would not interfere with Western expansionism.

The idea of boarding schools, however, did not start in the late 1800s with Pratt. Boarding schools for Indian students were proposed a century earlier by Reverend Eleazer Wheelock, a missionary who believed the only way for Indian children to abandon their abhorrent culture was to remove them from their parents. Lieutenant Pratt took Wheelock's proposal a step further by taking Indian children away from their tribal environment younger and keeping them longer. His beliefs were similar to Commissioner of Indian Affairs J.D.C. Atkins, who said, "The first step to be taken toward civilization, toward teaching the Indians. . . is to teach them in English. Education should seek the disintegration of the tribe" (Hirschfelder & de Montano 1993, 95). Language is the glue that binds a culture. Therefore, forcing Indian children to learn English away from their tribal environment would speed the process of assimilation.

In 1882, the federal government authorized the use of abandoned military forts for the schools, and military officers as the teachers. In just three short years, there were 177 government schools across the United States. By 1913, the government was operating 233 Indian day schools on reservations, 76 boarding schools on reservations, and 35 boarding schools off reservation.

Pratt founded the Carlisle School for Indians. This school and others like it attempted to wipe out all remnants of Indian culture, and in the process sexual, physical, and emotional abuse often occurred. *In the White Man's Image* (2007), a documentary film about the early boarding schools, Pratt's treatment of Indian children was well portrayed.

The experiment in social engineering carried out in many of these institutions, called boarding schools and later on industrial Schools, may have produced a different kind of Indian but not one that anyone could call a "true American." More often than not, institutionalized Indian children were caught in limbo as whites held onto outdated stereotypes and as Indians on Indian country distrusted them. "Educated" Indians felt as though they did not belong in the tribal world or the world of whites. The outcome was often a cycle of dependency and despair.

In the documentary film *Our Spirits Don't Speak English* (2008), adult Indians who experienced institutionalization in the twentieth century spoke about their treatment as children. While their treatment may not have been as regimented and as physically abusive as Pratt's schools, the sexual and emotional abuse created deep-seated trauma with which many of these adults continue to wrestle.

How many children attended boarding schools is difficult to ascertain. From government documents, we can speculate that between 1880 and 1950, fully two-thirds of all Indian people educated were educated in the boarding school system and at the 132 on-reservation day schools (Fleming 2003).

Overall, most schools were unsuccessful in their goal of making the *Indian-ness* disappear. While some Indian graduates may have prospered, most did not. "When we enter the schools we at least know we are Indian. We come out half red and half white," stated the Sioux medicine man John Lame Deer (Hirschfelder and de Montano 1993, 96). In no other institution have there been efforts to change Indians in its most brutal form than in these schools. Unfortunately, more civilization and *Americanization* occurred with very little education.

If these schools were to be successful in culturally changing Indian children, Congress would have to be willing to commit the financial resources necessary. By 1901, partly because Indians like the Hopi hid their children from being taken and also because Congress was unwilling to provide additional funds, the number of Indians placed in boarding schools declined significantly.

In short, while the endeavors of Pratt and others did little to encourage Indians to adopt the newly created national identity, they did signal government of the need to create more innovative legislation that would not only force assimilation but also make it possible to solve another part of the Indian problem, the economic one.

As discussed in Chapter 4, the chief provisions of the General Allotment Act (GAA) focused on *Civilizing, Christianizing,* and *Americanizing* Indians, much like the boarding schools. Political elites believed that by merely accepting an individual piece of land, Indians would be less Indian, and thus closer to being white. The main idea behind the GAA was that individual ownership would create pride, self-interest, and a healthy selfishness, leading to Christianity and civilization. Note that all three of these characteristics have to do with self: *individual ownership, self-interest, healthy selfishness.* Incorporation of Indians into economic and political structures could occur only as *individuals.* This suggests that national identity is highly dependent upon inner-directedness, rather than other-directedness. Obviously, this is a major problem for collectives; most collectives, if not all, have little if any concept of *self.* The consciousness of collectives is directed to the collective, not to the self. For example, one such ceremony discussed in Chapter 3 that exemplifies a sense of strong collectives is the Potlatch or giveaways. Potlatchs formed the core of native spirituality and ensured that no one in traditional societies would go hungry. In reaction to these giveaways, the federal government began a campaign to eradicate the Potlatch, stating that Indians should keep their stuff for themselves, rather than give it away. Government hoped that a sense of *healthy selfishness* would develop with the eradication of giveaways, but it did not.

Making the Potlatch illegal coupled with the implementation of the GAA did not culturally transform Indians either. However, while the GAA did accomplish a massive decrease of land held by Indian nations and shifted tribally controlled land to individual Indians and whites, its implementation created a more sinister plan. The government put in place what many Indians describe as a form of genetic engineering. Since the function of the GAA was to expedite the process of civilization by unilaterally dissolving Indians' collectively held reservation land and distributing this land to individual Indians, government needed to know who was Indian. Therefore, the idea of "blood quantum" or "degree of Indian blood" was adopted. Each Indian that could document they were one-fourth or more Indian would be eligible for an allotment of land.

In both races, African and Indigenous, Euro-Americans used a "degree of blood" to define Indians and African. In the Journal of Anthropology (2011) Ryan W. Schmidt traces the original use of "blood" during colonial times and during the GAA and the IRA.

> The earliest use of "blood" to trace genealogy occurred in precolonial governments of North America. For example, Virginia in 1705 came to a legal definition of "mixed blood" by coining the term "mulatto" for those individuals with at least 1/8 blood African ancestry or 1/2 Indian ancestry. "Colored" and "mulatto" were defined by a number of states in colonial times, usually for the purposes of restricting and/or limiting civil and/or property rights.

While the blood quantum for African ancestry is no longer used to define who is of African descent, the degree of Indian blood continues to be used today, and continued to be used in federal Indian policies that followed the GAA.

Still bent on creating a civil society out of savage societies, government created the Indian Reorganization Act of 1934 (IRA). In order to distribute the necessary resources to tribal governments, federal government needed to generate a *census* of Indians. If tribes wanted funding, they would have to make a "list of their Indians." This was referred to as enrollments.

By modernizing tribal government, federal government could better "work" with them and better control them. Once again, the federal government assumed that structures made the people. However, the transfer of power from the population (citizens) to political elites (governance), similar to how U.S. cities govern, did not occur to any large degree in Indian nations, leaving many contemporary tribal governments with a structure that incorporates both modern and traditional ways. More importantly, many Indians refused to enroll their children fearing removal or institutionalization. Subsequently, the major consequences of these policies and the institutionalization of Indian children brought more confusion among many Indians and whites as to what it means to be *Indian.*

WHAT IS AN INDIAN?

As political philosopher Charles Taylor (1992) noted, the creation of an identity is crucially dependent upon relations with others of the identity they desire or of the identity they were born into. Consequently, the institutionalization of Indian children made it difficult for Indians to sustain the identity they were born into, and furthered the creation of a new identity more associated with that of ethnic groups. Therefore, the distinction between ethnic groups and nations is an important distinction for a number of key reasons. In his book *American Indian Politics*, David E. Wilkins points out succinctly why Indians are not minorities. First, tribal peoples are the original inhabitants of North America, and "they are nations in the most fundamental sense of the word" (2011, 33); thus, giving Indians rights and control over specific territories where they do wield some control or jurisdiction is crucial. Second, with the formation of the United States, over 500 political compacts and treaties were negotiated. No other American racial/ethnic group entered into *Treaty making*; this confirms a nation-to-nation relationship. Moreover, the rights of tribes are not subject to the U.S. Constitution as are the rights of ethnic groups. A third feature that differentiates indigenous people from ethnic groups is the *trust doctrine*. Since Chief Justice Marshall's Supreme Court's decision in 1830, the United States recognizes Indian tribes as *domestic dependent nations* under U.S. protection with the United States acting as guardians and Indians as wards. As Vine Deloria Jr. stated:

> The trust responsibility of the federal government toward the Indian tribes is mandated by the fact that Indians are extra constitutional. No constitutional protections exist for Indians in either a tribal or an individual sense, and hence the need for special rules and regulations, special administrative discretionary authority, and special exemptions. This special body of law replaces the constitutional protections granted to other members of American society (DeLoria 1985, 241).

The plenary power of Congress clearly separates Indian nations from ethnic groups as well. Congressional plenary power means Congress has unlimited, absolute, complete, and preemptive power. As recently as 1978, the Supreme Court held that "Congress has plenary authority to legislate for the Indian tribes in all matters, including their form of government" (435 U.S. 313, 319). Moreover, while there is not a Bureau of African American Affairs or a Bureau of Chicano Affairs, there is a Bureau of Indian Affairs with a long and heavily controlling arm. In short, indigenous peoples have all the characteristics of a national minority; they share a common language, religion, culture, and other identifying characteristics, and a relationship to a particular territory, but are subjugated by a dominant culture and society and continue to be a dependent nation within a nation. In addition, they have a different worldview, consisting of a custodial and nonmaterialistic attitude toward land

and natural resources, and want to pursue a separate development compared with that imposed by the dominant society and those of ethnic groups. While ethnic groups may have some of the characteristics listed above, the legal and historical reality separates them from the various Indian nations within the United States. More importantly, there is not an African American law or Chicano law, but there is Federal Indian law that guides and controls virtually everything Indian nations do within the confines of their territory.

Separate from Indians being defined as members of Indian nations, by the late 1960s when "Red Power" was taking shape and because of Indian urbanization, Indian government homes, and Indian boarding schools, Indian identity began to evolve into diverse categories. Jack Forbes (1981) lists four categories that are useful in understanding identity differences and self-identification:

1. Traditional Nationalists: Represents values, principles, and approaches of an indigenous perspective that accepts no compromise with colonial structures; individuals who feel that their nationality is Indian.

2. Secular nationalists: Represents incomplete or unfulfilled Indigenous perspective stripped of its spiritual element and oriented almost solely toward confronting the colonial structures. These are predominantly Indians that have had the urban experience and who may share the traditions and ceremonies but whose identity is clearly political and whose activities are directed toward goals of tribal sovereignty.

3. Tribal pragmatists: Represents an interest-based calculation and perspective that merges Indian and mainstream values toward the integration of native communities within colonial structures, many of which are Christians.

4. Americans of Indian Descent (Racial minority): Represents a perspective completely separate from indigenous cultures and supportive of the colonial structures that are the sole source of native identification. These individuals "often share the values of their white middle-class peers and oppose Indian nationalism."

There are clear examples of each of the above categories. For example, a traditional nationalist is one who defines themselves through their tribe, not as an American, not as an American Indian, or any of the other various identities, but as Lakota, Navajo, Hopi, and so forth. These are Indians who have a clear idea of who they are and ones that may not have experienced any of the institutionalization processes discussed earlier.

A secular nationalist is a citizen of an Indian nation but one whose activities are more clearly defined as political, not necessarily religious. Some American Indian Movement (AIM) members or native activists might identify themselves as such. Research does show that many Indian activists may have experienced institutionalization or resided in the urban area and forced to straddle two worlds.

Tribal pragmatists are often those individuals or collectives that understand the importance of working with the federal and state governments, especially on economic, political, and social issues. Certain tribes, like the Navajo Nation, that have an abundance of natural resources must be pragmatic in their decisions. They know very well how the federal government reacts should they choose not to negotiate. Through Oral history, the relocation of Navajo people in 1864, described as the *Long Walk,* is certainly kept alive. In addition, the Navajo faced relocation once again during the 1974 Settlement Act, discussed earlier.

Finally, the fourth category, Americans of Indian descent, are largely those individuals that have little to no contact with their tribe's traditions and ceremonies and by all accounts are assimilated by choice or by consequences. This category might include members of the Society of American Indians (SAI) who experienced the early boarding schools. SAI members, consisting of highly professional Indians, believed their allegiance should be firstly to the United States. It might also include institutionalized Indians who chose for various reasons to define themselves as such. A more recent group is that of Mexican American or Chicano populations. There is no denying that the Mexican American heritage is closely connected to the Indio cultural roots and to the Iberian culture of Spain. This dual connectedness provides Mexicans or Chicanos with an opportunity to identify more with their Indian roots and less with their Spanish or Mexican heritage. On the 2000 Census, the broad Latin American Indian grouping was replaced by the individual tribal groupings of "Central American Indian," "Mexican American Indian," "South American Indian," and "Spanish American Indian." According to the Census Bureau, among the top 10 tribes, Mexican American Indians as a category were fourth, following the Cherokee (819,105); Navajo (332,129); and Choctaw (195,764). While there is not a Mexican American Indian nation per se, certainly not one that is federally recognized, this can be misleading. Nonetheless, this group is a racial minority and fits the fourth category.

In large part, the actions and policies of the U.S. Government purposefully encouraged, if not forced, Indians to embrace the fourth category, rather than the category of tribal nationalism. Had termination been fully implemented, it is likely all Indians would have been forced to define themselves as American, period, and be classified as a racial minority. However, that did not happen.

Obviously, the category of tribal nationalists and secular nationalists creates problems for dominant society, dominant culture, and the power holders, specifically when nationalists focus on increased sovereignty, as they did in the 1970s, under the guidance of the AIM.

ACTIVITIES THAT REINFORCE THE MAKING OF A TRIBAL IDENTITY

AIM organizers understood early what could happen if they could validate their activities within the minds of the large urban Indian population and those Indians living on the reservations. Therefore, one of the first goals of the organizers was not only to discard previous images of Indians, and in the process expose the true nature of the federal government, but also to facilitate the creation of a new tribal identity, one that is more relative to the experience of Indians. Old stereotypical Indian images needed to be shattered and replaced by a more respectful and historically correct image. Therefore, one of the first tactics of Indian activists was to demand a change in the names of schools, universities, and of Indian mascots. The use of native names, images, and symbols was a racist practice, not *honoring* Indians, as university officials stated. As author, professor, and AIM activist Glenn Morris stated, people should remember that an honor isn't honor when it parts the honorer's lips; it is born when it is accepted in the honoree's ear (Churchill 1996, 439). Moreover, as Mihesuah asks in her book, *American Indian Stereotypes and Realities*, how can it be said that Indians are being honored by portraying them "with their drunkenness, dyed turkey feathers and sloppy face paint, screeching war hoops and spasmodic dance steps that belong to no tribe" (1996, 17). Mihesuah examines how these and many other stereotypes reinforce the idea that Indians lack any ability to govern themselves.

Stereotypes not only reinforce the idea of dependency, but also have the capacity to affect academic performance, self-esteem of Native Americans, and contribute heavily to a number of issues Native Americans confront on a daily basis. However, before much would change, these images would need to be defined as false and recognized as having been created by the federal government and larger society to justify and rationalize the treatment of American Indians. Activists and Native scholars realized this, and set in motion activities that would address these issues and facilitate change.

Unlike the "education" received in boarding schools that were in the hands of whites, and purposefully administered to create a certain type of Indian, activists, scholars, and American Indians believed that Natives should be in charge of their own education. That is to say, the creation of an education by Indians and for Indians that more accurately portrays Indians. This education should not omit the contributions of American Indians to America in any one of the disciplines, whether history, culture, or politics, and should be inclusive of an indigenous perspective. According to scholar Elizabeth Cook-Lynn, considered by many scholars to be the Mother of Native American Studies, the goal of classes on American Indians should be Indian nationalism and sovereignty. If classes on Native Americans assist students with learning the unique histories of indigenous peoples, as well as their unique federal status, recognize stereotypes and bias in writings and conversations, understand the manifestations of colonization, and how these impact tribal nations, there is a greater possibility that an Indian identity closely matched with Indian tribal culture will develop. The consequence of discussing Indian culture and ceremonies in nonpolitical terms, and excluding the process of cultural genocide, omits a large portion of what it means to be Indian, and continues the creation of identity frames, or lens, with which images of Indians are manufactured. When relationships between images, situations, and policies are not addressed within the context of sovereignty and tribal nationalism, images of Indians remain the same.

For example, photographs of Indians rebelling during the Occupation of Wounded Knee in 1973 disrupted passive images of Indians carefully orchestrated by government and held by most Americans. Image is ideology adapted to political uses, suggests Kelly (1980). Incidents such as occupations, riots, protests, and fish-ins worked to create a level of cognitive dissonance in larger society. Cognitive dissonance occurs when an individual's perception does not fit what they see or what they have learned. Consequently, many Americans, including some Indians, may have chosen to deny or ignore these new images and stick to their earlier perceptions of Indians. Most people do not discard images the first time they do not match what they know. Most of us adjust the image to fit our worldview rather than adjust our worldview. Nonetheless, Native militants were able to use this mismatch to point out the hypocrisy of the federal government.

Naturally, the federal government was very aware of AIM using identity politics to mobilize Indians and non-Indians. At the 1973 Academy Awards, Marlon Brando asked Sacheen Littlefeather, an Apache actor, to respectfully decline his Oscar in view of the treatment of Indians in the film industry, and at the Wounded Knee Occupation. Brando identified with the politics of Indians, and government, fearing the potential role of identity politics in the rebellion, quickly removed media from Wounded Knee. Consequently, America was solely dependent upon government's interpretation of the image of a rebellious Indian.

The literature on identity politics and its ability to facilitate change is not new. In 1980, Peter du Preez wrote *The Politics of Identity.* du Preez examined white South Africa; however there is much to extrapolate in regard to Natives and Americans. *In Democracy on Trial*, (1995) author Jean Bethke Elshtain writes that the politics of identity splits society. When the reaction and response of members to politics is influenced or dependent upon race, class, religion, ethnicity, culture, or sexual preference, the common identity becomes fragile, suggests Elshtain. While Elshtain says nothing about Native Americans, it is obvious her response of Indians displacing their forced identity with a tribal identity would work against the common interest of U.S. civil society.

Therefore, the "we" of collective identities is a collection of events that are similar in certain respects and different in other respects. The common event for many urban Indians is that of removal and relocation, either through adoption, foster-care, relocation legislation, or in boarding schools, churches, government schools, and, more recently, prison. The difference is that these events did not happen at the same age, the same place, and by the same agents. Furthermore, many of these forced relocations had different consequences on the people experiencing them, thus increasing the possible methods individual Indians use to create their understanding of tribal identity. In other words, to achieve a consensus about what it means to be Indian, the collective draws upon the shared experiences of Indians. However, this process must include *tribalization*; that is, as Stephen Cornell defines it, the process of how tribes have become what they are today. That process varies considerably, and therefore so does the process of creating a tribal identity tied to any one of the numerous Indian nations. Indians who experience the obliteration of their Indian-ness, feelings of invisibility, or who see the "vanishing Indian" perspective applied, understand this best.

There is a belief that if an Indian is full-blooded they are "more Indian" than an Indian who is one-fourth or one-half. When a white person asks an Indian how much Indian they are, they are legitimizing what the federal government put in place without understanding the complexity of Indian history, of which they often know little. The concept of full-bloods versus half-bloods and so forth is not a concept that whites incorporate when evaluating themselves or other whites. In a society where individualism is valued, Americans can detach themselves from the interests of the United States, and it does not make them less American, even though some Americans like to think they are more American than others, by the size of the flags they fly, for example. However, within a collective, a tribal identity cannot be detached from the "real" interests of the tribe. When Indians focus on individual interests, their tribal identity is at risk. Moreover, we cannot assume that all interests of all tribes are the same all of the time.

Indian American or American Indian?

Most Americans *think* they know Indians, but this identity is one that Americans hold because they have been socialized to believe them. Socialization effectively replaces force in the governing of society. That is to say, government did not need to force whites to think of Indians as savages and so forth; it merely gave whites something for conforming to these sets of beliefs. The reward or payoff used to be land; now it is access to resources, a feeling of self-righteousness or superiority. For American Indians, the very essence of what it means to be Indian conflicts with what it means to be an American, particularly since what it means to be an American is a political identity free of any cultural traits, etc. Most Americans believe it is human nature to be greedy, to be an individual, to own, control, and exploit nature. American Indians believe nature put Indians in nature to temper the behavior of groups bent on destroying it. Various Indian ceremonies and activities promote an indigenous interpretation of human nature that is often at odds with the interpretation of what it means to be American. To what extent this indigenous interpretation takes hold in the minds of Indians is up to the numerous "I's" who are seeking an understanding of who they are, coupled with the responses and reactions of government and larger society.

Therefore, what it means to be an American is lacking for many Native Americans, mostly because it is void of any reference to Indian heritage, tradition, and customs of which are numerous. Because of America's ideological tie to individualism, competition, and materialism, there continues to be a level of nonacceptance of those values within most Indians, often making their self-identity less American and more Indian.

Similar to Indians, the newly hyphenated Americans demonstrate that many of them are searching for their heritage, a link to their past, a history that provides traces of whom they are. For American Indians, the past, if interpreted with an indigenous perspective, has its greatest potential of explaining the present and the future. Policies of assimilation, removal, relocation, termination, and so forth, failed to conquer the descendants of the original inhabitants of the United States and thus to firmly change their identity. However, as long as Indians have all the characteristics of a national minority, yet a legal definition that separates them from other national minorities and other Americans, many of them will continue to feel pulled between two worlds, particularly for those Indians who live off tribal land.

Perhaps Lipset (1996) was right when he wrote that American exceptionalism is a double-edged sword mainly because of paradoxes within American culture that tend to shape an identity that is rooted in ideology rather than history. He further states that people will only dissolve the political bonds that connect them and create a new one to which the laws of Nature and of Nature's God entitles them. We know that Indian political consciousness has increased owing to certain activities of Indian and non-Indian activists and has thus created an environment that makes it possible for the revival and creation of an Indian identity determined by Indians rather than government, as propelled by AIM and other Indian activists.

There is little doubt that the spirit of activism demonstrated by AIM and discussed in Chapter 7 had a fundamental impact on Native people not only in furthering a tribal cultural identity but also in furthering levels of tribal sovereignty. Within the United States, social movement theorists have demonstrated that the expansion of democracy has occurred most often through social movement activities. For example, without the Civil Rights Movement, there is little doubt the Civil Rights Act and the repeal of Jim Crow Laws would have occurred (McAdam 1982; Button 1978). In addition, we can say with some certainty that without the activities of Native activists and tribal governments, it is unlikely a key piece of

Indian legislation that affects identity, the Indian Child Welfare Act (ICWA) 1978, would have passed.

In 1968, the Devils Lake Sioux of North Dakota requested the assistance of the Association of the American Indian Affairs (AAIA) to stop the removals and placements of Indian children. In 1969, the AAIA conducted a study showing widespread removal of Indian children. By 1974, Native protest and AAIA activity led to a 1974 hearing before the Senate Subcommittee on Indian affairs. At the hearing, Senator James Aborezk of South Dakota said, "Unwarranted removal of children from their homes is common in Indian communities. For decades Indian parents and their children have been at the mercy of arbitrary or abusive action of local, State, Federal, and private agency officials" (U.S. Senate Hearing). Because of this hearing, an additional study by AAIA, and a 1977 hearing of the Senate Select Committee on Indian Affairs, ICWA passed.

In its investigation of Indian children's removal, Congress found that State actors removed between 25 and 35 percent of all Indian children nationwide, placing the majority of those children in non-Indian homes. With the passage of ICWA, standards were passed for the placement of Indian children in foster and adoptive homes, and provided tribes and families the opportunity to be involved in the placement of children, rather than allowing states and individuals to take Indian children without the approval of tribal governments. The law ensures that removal of Indian children is necessitated by some harm faced by the child, rather than fulfilling some goals of cultural transformation. If the child is to be removed, they should be placed first within the Indian family, within the child's tribal affiliation, or with another Indian family. This ensures to some degree that the child is able to maintain their tribal identity and is not severed from their cultural heritage.

While there continue to be problems with the law, ICWA has given tribal governments a voice in deciding where their children go, if anywhere. When Indian children stay with their tribe, their identity is structured to the needs of the tribe rather than to the needs of larger American society, thus creating the conditions for Indians to have a firm sense of who they are, and diminishes feelings that they do not belong in either world. Moreover, the passage of ICWA signifies an increase in tribal sovereignty, something that clearly affects the future of Native peoples.

ICWA is but one example of what Native protests in conjunction with tribal demands are capable of accomplishing. In the following chapter, we discuss the kind of tactics Indian activists used to gain more political power. No doubt, many of these tactics led to the creation of Indian legislation by Indians and for Indians.

QUESTIONS FOR DISCUSSION:

1) What is the American Creed, and how can it be said that it is a political identity largely free of any cultural identity?

2) For American Indians, the very essence of what it means to be Indian conflicts with what it means to be an American. Explain what this means.

3) If an education omits the history of American Indians in an American History class, what are the consequences? Do you think all of the cultures of America should be included in American traditional courses?

4) How does the use of American Indian stereotypes not only reinforce the idea of dependency but also have the capacity to affect academic performance, self-esteem of Native Americans?

5) In what ways did the passage of ICWA increase tribal sovereignty?

CHAPTER SEVEN

INDIGENOUS MOVEMENT POLITICS

They promised us that we could fish. . .as "long as the mountain stands, the grass grows green and the sun shines." But now the State of Washington has declared the steel-head trout a "white man's fish." They must think the steel-head swam over behind the *Mayflower* (Steiner 1968, 55).

The framers of the U.S. Constitution recognized the cultural diversity of American society, but they could not have foreseen the influence diversity would later play in government. The American system is based on interest group politics, where a number of Americans form an interest group in an effort to put pressure on government to get their interests met. These diverse interests necessitate the creation of a number of *factions*. In theory, as long as there are a number of factions with diverse interests putting pressure on policy makers, it is less likely these factions would become one large faction and overthrow economic elites whose interests are less diverse. The propertyless majority, as Madison pointed out in Federalist No. 10, must not be allowed to make common cause against the propertied class and its established social order. That is to say, the greater the variety of interests, the more factions and the more difficult it would be for a mass majority (one large faction) to act in union.

Today, interest groups provide individuals with numerous channels besides voting to shape legislation. Simply put, *interest groups* or *pressure groups* (pluralism) are groups of people who organize to pursue a common interest, *passion,* by applying pressure on the political process. The largest and probably the most powerful of U.S. interest groups are economic interest groups, groups that seek greater private profits for their members. Other interest groups are often organized around religious, social, or political concerns and often focus on collective interests. A few examples of interest groups are Common Cause, the National Organization of Women, the National Rifle Association, the National Congress of American Indians, and the National Indian Youth Council. Some of these organizations are working not only on collective interests but also on private interests, those interests that only their organization would receive. American Indian interest groups work toward a collective interest of either a specific tribe or all tribes.

Regardless of their respective diverse interests, all interest groups recognize the need to put pressure on government through an assortment of activities. The most common form of tactic is lobbying. Lobbyists are hired by the interest group to directly or indirectly influence legislation specific to the interests of the group they represent. Their activities include lobbying a congressional member to vote for or against a particular bill, or possibly sponsoring a bill, raising monetary support for congressional campaigns, writing letters to Congress expressing the groups' interests, and aligning the group with other groups with similar goals and interests.

While interest groups on the whole use institutional tactics to get their interests met, some groups use other types of activities defined as *noninstitutional or nonconventional.* Noninstitutional tactics are those tactics outside of the accepted institutional forum. Strikes, boycotts, demonstrations, protests, and other forms of disruptive tactics are usually identified as nonconventional. When an interest group uses primarily noninstitutional or nonconventional tactics, they are viewed as engaging in confrontational or movement politics.

Therefore, it is fair to say that a social movement is an interest group, meaning it is made up of people with a collective interest and it also attempts to influence policies in its direction. However, what separates social movements from interest groups, among other things, are the types of strategies used to achieve their goals. A useful definition of a social movement is taken from Doug McAdam's political opportunity model. McAdam suggests that social movements are *"rational attempts by excluded groups to mobilize sufficient political leverage to advance collective interests through non-institutional means"* (McAdam 1982, 37).

Consequently, social movements are interest groups, but interest groups are not necessarily social movements. Those individuals engaged in social movement activities see themselves as excluded from the political process and those individuals in interest groups see the process as legitimate and useful for their purposes. Social movements often become interest groups; for example, the Women's Movement became the National Organization of Women (NOW), or the Civil Rights Movement became various interest groups like the National Association for the Advancement of Colored Peoples (NAACP), which defends the rights of African Americans. These groups got involved in movement or confrontational politics when they realized their interests could be better achieved using the political process and specifically after the barriers that were once in place excluding them were removed.

Interest groups can also become social movements, particularly when the group recognizes that using conventional strategies will not further their interests. Moreover, they see themselves as excluded from the political process. An example of a group moving from an interest group to a movement and back to an interest group is the National Indian Youth Council (NIYC). When Indians realized using conventional tactics was futile in getting their demands met, they pursued strategies described as militant or confrontational politics. Some key members of the NIYC eventually joined the American Indian Movement (AIM) and pushed the level of militancy even more. The NIYC did not stop using interest group strategies; rather, they aligned their interests with AIM and began using noninstitutional and institutional strategies.

Another key difference between interest groups and movement politics is how American society reacts to them. American society has historically embraced interest group politics largely because they use the political channels open to them, voting, letter writing, signing petitions, and so forth, and do not embrace disruptive, confrontational strategies. Moreover, Americans are socialized to use these types of strategies rather than confrontational strategies. When a group uses other more disruptive types of strategies such as protest, demonstrations, occupations, economic boycotts, and certainly tactics that entail a use of violence, Americans often become less supportive. That is because Americans who use the system see government as legitimate, are taught to support the political process, use the designated channels to get their demands met, and their demands are often met.

The irony of this socialization process is that democracy in the United States has expanded greatly as a result of social movement activity and not so much as a result of interest group activities. For example, the efforts of the labor movement severely expanded the voice of the worker and pushed government to institute a number of policies that protected workers, and created the conditions whereby workers could increase their political power. Unlike in the past, they could now create unions. They could now strike when before striking was illegal. The Women's Movement also expanded the level of democracy of women in a number of ways, specifically by garnering the vote for women, pushing for equality in the work force, and ensuring reproductive choice. Finally, most Americans would acknowledge that without the Civil Rights Movement it is highly unlikely that Black Americans, women, and other minorities would have the political and economic clout they have today. These various movements worked to increase democracy for those Americans who may have been citizens but were largely excluded from full participation.

During the period that many of these activities took place, the United States experienced a level of social movement activity unparalleled since the depression decade of the 1930s. The Civil Rights Movement gained momentum, the Antiwar Movement hit the street, university students challenged restrictions on the right to free speech, many Americans showed their discontent with the war in Vietnam, and numerous people participated in riots in the urban areas. It was amidst this turmoil that American Indians began to more intensely resist the policies of the U.S. Government. But how did Indians move *from hopeless submission to hopeful noncompliance?* What set of factors facilitated the increased rights of American Indians?

THE EARLY YEARS OF INSURGENCY

In the 1960s, Indians numbered close to 1.5 million nationwide, and were scattered across the states in approximately 500 tribes that were at the time recognized as Indian Tribes. They had an unemployment rate escalating in some areas as high as 90 percent, an increasing birthrate, plus a large population under 19 years of age. With conditions like these, Indians realized they needed to alter the grim statistics plaguing their lives and believed the only way they could turn these statistics around was to achieve some form of self-government. Merely demanding it had not proven to be effective, possibly taking it would.

It was during this period that a new type of Indian materialized, ready to challenge the federal government and its controlling agent, the Bureau of Indian Affairs (BIA), in a more militant way. Consequently, out of a response to a lack of participation on the part of Indians in initiating and controlling government programs, a number of indigenous organizations began to spring up. Indian groups that used similar tactics as other American interest groups began to form.

Membership of early American Indian interest groups was entirely white. While the Friends of Indians and the Association on American Indian Affairs were good advocates for Indian interests, Indians began to realize Indian interests could only be achieved by Indians.

The first successful attempt by Indians to form a national political organization (interest group) was the Society of American Indians (SAI). The SAI was a progressive group made up of professional men and women who were doctors, lawyers, ministers, anthropologists, and bureaucrats, largely educated and acculturated in the early Indian boarding schools. The group focused on education, legislation, and membership. One member, a Seneca anthropologist, Arthur C. Parker, believed that the future of Indians was with the white race. "To survive at all [the Indian] must become as other men, a contributing self-sustaining member of society. No nation can afford to permit any person or body of people within it to exist in a condition at variance with the ideal of that nation" (Hertzberg 1982, 63).

At this time, approximately 13 percent of school-age Indian children were in boarding schools. The SAI was a very small group of Indians who were "successes" of the boarding school experience. However, most Indians still lived on reservations and did not see the world as did the SAI. In addition, the interests of many Indians were not aligned with the interests of the SAI. Consequently, the SAI was short-lived.

The next interest group organized in reaction to the Indian Reorganization Act. The American Indian Federation (AIF) was founded primarily in 1934 to reverse the Indian New Deal and abolish the BIA. Much of its rhetoric appealed to the right wing of the 1930s that were also against Roosevelt's New Deal initiatives. The AIF was not widely supported, and by the mid-1940s it was no longer an organization. However, another Indian group was ready to take the lead and they had a much broader base of support: the National Congress of American Indians (NCAI).

The first event NCAI organized was a success. In November of 1944, it held a large convention in Denver. Seventy-five delegates from 50 reservations gathered. Similar to the SAI some of the delegates were well educated, professionals and graduates of boarding schools. Others were veterans having served in the Second World War. A key difference of the NCAI from the two earlier organizations was that the NCAI focused on treaty rights and tribal cultures. The NCAI expanded their interests to include practical aspects of politics such as legal aid for tribes, voting rights, and land and cultural issues (Cornell 1988).

There is no doubt that the NCAI laid the foundation for the creation of a more organized and militant national Indian movement. The first large national organized Indian event occurred in 1961. More than 500 Native Americans from 67 tribes met in Chicago. The purpose of this meeting was to demand from the Kennedy Administration cultural survival and a preservation of their land base (New York Times Index). From this meeting a Declaration of Indian Purpose was generated, which stated:

> We believe in the inherent rights of all people to retain spiritual and cultural values and that the free exercise of these values is necessary to the normal development of any people. Indians exercised this inherent right to live their own lives for thousands of years before the white man came and took their lands. When Indians speak of the continent they yielded, they are not referring only to the loss of some millions of acres in real estate. They have in mind that the land supported a universe of things they knew, valued, and loved. With that continent gone, except for the few parcels they still retain, the basis of life is precariously held, but they mean to hold the scraps and parcels as earnestly as any small nation or ethnic group was ever determined to hold to identity and survival (Witt and Steiner 1972, 216).

While many of the demands of the various tribes were cohesive, the meeting exposed a division among the more traditional members and the younger urban members. The younger and more militant members such as Clyde Warrior, an Oklahoma Ponca, thought that the declaration may have spelled out their desires but to believe participation in federal policies was the key to change was ignoring Indian history. He suggested a more aggressive policy needed to be implemented. Several months later Clyde Warrior and other younger members met in New Mexico and formed the NIYC (Josephy 1971). The NIYC set the lead for which many of the organizations followed. They began to link members of the aggrieved population into a more organized campaign of mass political action. More importantly, the NIYC distinguished itself from other organizations by making a more visible shift toward activism. It called for the end to racism, ethnocentrism, and paternalism characteristic of many federal policies. They demanded a new role for Native Americans in determining policies that affected their lives—one that would not be given to them but one they would create (Josephy 1971). The NIYC thus distinguished itself from the strict definition of interest groups and began to use tactics that would later define them as a social movement.

From 1961 through 1968, the NIYC and various tribes initiated many events directed at the federal government in an effort to alert the administration that a new Indian had arrived. Some events brought tribes together such as the meeting in September of 1962 in North Carolina. At this meeting, 75 tribal leaders met to unify their grievances. Consequently, the National Congress called for an emergency meeting of 80 representatives to begin reshaping Indian policy.

There were other events staged to increase Indian land base. The Sioux in Wisconsin sought to regain 800,000 acres of land ceded in 1837; the Seminoles in Florida and Oklahoma sought to regain 32 million acres; the Ottawa Tribe in Michigan demanded $938,291 for land sold to the government; and 40 Indians stopped logging operations as part of a long-standing dispute over rights to 19,000 acres. Tribal jurisdiction was challenged in other events. In South Dakota, tribes and various church groups opposed a referendum to bring dual federal/tribal law system under the state jurisdiction. The American Indian National Congress, a new interest group, supported the end of federal control of Indians in the state of Washington.

Many other groups and individual Indians called for an increase in cultural and civil rights. For example, the Iroquois in New York demanded the return of wampum belts from a New York museum; in San Francisco, Native Americans declared textbooks slanderous to Indians; Mohawks boycotted school board elections in an effort to seek their right to vote; and, after protesting their right to travel freely on U.S./Canadian border and blocking a bridge, the Canadian police held 41 Indians.

These types of events illustrate a change in the direction of Native Americans. They signified a new nationalism and an awareness promoted particularly by the NIYC. No longer were Indians willing to sit passively while government orchestrated their destiny. There continued to be small protests to stock reduction, methods of education, and other programs. However, these protests occurred in individual tribes and had very little support from other tribes or from nonindigenous groups. Consequently, a resurgent nationalism did not develop at this time. Indians were still in a position of making very little progress toward changing the federal policies they individually or tribally opposed.

Within a few years, all of this changed. The single greatest change in the structure of the Native American community in the 1960s was the mass migration to urban centers. This migration had enormous political ramifications. Either under the relocation programs or on their own volition, migration into the urban areas provided Indian organizations with thousands of Indians who, if mobilized, could mount an effective insurgency. In this respect, urbanization benefited Indian organizations. Yet, in another respect, Indian organizations were confronted with how the interests of Indians living in the cities could be linked with the interests of those living on reservations. Indians living on the reservations were isolated from the urban events of the sixties and additionally held rather narrow political interests. Motivating them to challenge federal policies would be a difficult but necessary task.

The American Indian Movement, an opposition group, undertakes this task. A small group of Indians that began to observe the rising activism of African and Hispanic Americans organized AIM. These urban Indians saw that their conditions were much worse than the general population, and worse than those minorities seeking change. Russell Means, an AIM activist and an urbanite at the time, said his involvement was generated by the realization of funds going to Blacks while Indians were virtually being overlooked (Means Interview 1988).

According to Means, the key to mobilizing Indians living on the reservation was to encourage them to continue resisting the BIA, a long-standing target of resistance, in conjunction with instilling a desire to return to their traditional customs. During the early stages of organizing, the newly developed groups were not completely clear as to the potential effects of motivating both sectors of the Indian population. "We just knew they had to be united," Means said (Means interview 1988). Getting the reservation Indians to recognize the need for change would come to be a major focus of the AIM. Migration made it possible to organize meetings and demonstrations easily. When AIM combines these individuals with a portion of the reservation population willing to resist poor policy making, Americans began to see the creation of a national social movement.

AIM organizers realized that the organization could not build their goals solely on the concerns of either urban or reservation Indians. Therefore, AIM clearly defined the grievances of urban and reservation Indians as one: self-determination. Broadly defined, self-determination served as the fundamental goal of the movement. AIM suggested that the problem facing all Indians was their lack of power to direct their destiny and change their conditions. Moreover, this issue provided AIM leaders with the ability to easily mobilize various segments of the Indian population. No Indian or non-Indian could deny the historical realities of Indians. The federal government had already generated leanings toward self-determination; it was just a matter of AIM defining the terms and forcing implementation.

Additionally and very important, AIM did not demand the dissolution of other organizations or interest groups. Using the courts and other less militant tactics such as monitoring legislative activities and other institutional activities were never fully relinquished or discouraged by the movement; all tactics were necessary. What made AIM successful and united was the comingling of actors.

Unforeseen by the federal government as a stimulus of native activism was a policy developed in the 1960s. This policy allowed for land once used by the military to revert to its original owners if the land was not in use. Many Indians saw this policy as an opportunity to announce their stance for Indian self-determination and rightfully claim much of the land defined by this policy. After all, Indians viewed themselves as the original owners of this land.

Out of response to the above policy, AIM initiated its first action in 1969: the occupation of Alcatraz Island.

> We want all Indians people to join with us. . .We are issuing this call in an attempt to unify all our Indian Brothers behind a common cause. . . We realize . . .that we are not getting anywhere fast by working alone as individual tribes. If we can gather together as brothers and come to a common agreement, we feel that we can be much more effective, doing things for ourselves, instead of having someone else doing it, telling us what is good for us (Josephy 1971, 187).

The objective of the occupation was twofold: first, to acquire Alcatraz and build a cultural center for Native Americans; second, use the occupation as a basis for launching a pan-Indian movement. The first objective was never realized, the second was. This dramatic opportunity captured national press coverage and brought to the attention of Indians as well as non-Indians that an insurgency was in the making. More importantly, it signaled the United States as to the arrival of AIM—a new kind of Indian.

The main objectives of the militant activists in AIM were to stop their land base from shrinking, re-familiarize themselves with their culture, and preserve the earth. To achieve these objectives, AIM did not reject the probability of using violence. If violence was necessary to achieve its goal, then violence became an acceptable strategy of AIM. After occupying the Island for 18 months, the leadership returned the land, but not without some loss; one of the principal Indian leaders was shot and killed by federal government. Because of Alcatraz, other occupations of land and buildings occurred; some resulted in violence and arrests. The following events reported in newspapers are a few of the activities that took place in cities across the United States:

> —Jane Fonda and over 100 Indians occupied Fort Lawton in Seattle in an attempt to make it into a cultural center, 72 people were arrested.
> —Eight Indians in New York City were arrested when they occupied Ellis Island and

demanded that the island be made into a living center of Indian culture.

—In Davis, California, an unused army base was seized and occupied by 75 Indians, who wanted to use it as a cultural center.

—In Los Angeles, 12 Indians locked themselves in a museum to protest an exhibition of their ancestral bones.

—In Minnesota, 35 Indians occupied an unused federal building stating that it be used as a cultural center.

—In North Dakota, the Sioux occupied a portion of the Black Hills, held a prayer vigil and planned to fast until the land was returned to them.

—And in Chicago over 80 Indians occupied the Nike Missile site in Chicago for 7 months to protest Indian housing in Chicago; 12 were arrested.

Numerous sit-ins were also a method used to bring attention to Indian causes. For example, in Colorado, a four-day sit-in was held demanding that the commissioner of the BIA resign. Consequently, nine protesters were jailed. In Cleveland, the police held eight Indians for demonstrating against the BIA. In Fort Totten, over 40 Indians took over the jail and staged a peaceful sit-in to protest police brutality. In addition, in North Carolina, the Lumbee staged a classroom sit-in to oppose the integration of schools.

Most of the events in the early part of the 1960s began with few participants and less violence. As the end of the 1960s neared, events became larger, and violence appeared with more frequency. At the same time, courts as a form of strategy were used infrequently, but not completely abandoned, even though Indians were becoming increasingly disenchanted with the outcomes of the court hearings. In almost all court claims during this and prior periods, government responded to land claims and other claims with money. Money no longer would suffice. The goals of the militant Indians shifted: they rejected large sums of money and demanded land instead.

Occupations, sit-ins, and large demonstrations thus signaled the government that the political current had begun to change. Grievances were taken from the courts and into the streets with much rapidity, further suggesting that to defy institutions from which they are excluded made little sense. To demand sovereignty by using nonconventional tactics was increasingly being embraced.

THE PEAK

In the 1970s, well past the peak of other protesting groups, the shape of the AIM began to change significantly; it became much more militant. How Indians in general viewed life, land,

and resources not only shaped the movement but also added to the epic confrontation between whites and Indians. Johansen and Maestas suggest that the rationalization of the accumulation of profits masks a clash between two fundamentally different worldviews:

> The Judea-Christian view is anthropocentric: the human race is charged (as reflected in the Biblical book Genesis) with dominating the natural world. The Native Americans view, on the other hand, meshes humankind with nature as part of its dominant ways. The European immigrants had a well-defined concept of wealth and private property, which fueled their ambitions for accumulation. . . native cultures, with a few exceptions, had no such concept (1979, 25–26).

Furthermore, Judea-Christian (protestant) beliefs center on the individual, while the ideas of Native Americans center on the communal values of the nation or clan. Again, the trait of individuality was strongly connected to ownership of property. Following the *Lockeian* view, private property was a natural right, but also the basis of civilized society. AIM organized several events that revealed differences in values between whites and Indians. For example, AIM asked the Cleveland Indian Baseball team and Pocatello Idaho University to drop its Indian mascot. Both institutions refused. Unlike Cleveland and Pocatello, Stanford students called for a change in the University mascot and Stanford complied. In a different case, the governor of Iowa ordered the remains of five graves taken off public display after a protest. These types of events were ones with which most non-Indians could empathize. Subsequently, these symbolic actions helped AIM in its effort to make Native Americans more conscious of the way non-Indians displayed Indians and their heritage. AIM hoped that this consciousness would encourage Indians to change their place in American society while not alienating non-Indians.

Consequently, during the 1970s, numerous suits were filed against the federal government. Most of these suits had to do with the return of land. In 1972, 300 Indians filed a major suit. This suit demanded that the land claims reopen so that claims regarding leasing and gambling by tribes could be pursued. In few cases government responded positively. In most of these cases, money continued to be given instead of land. For example, the Acoma Pueblo in New Mexico were awarded a $6.1-million out-of-court settlement when they originally sought $2.5 million; the Osage in Oklahoma received $13.2 million for 28 million acres; and the Nez Perce in Idaho won $2,119,071 for land they sought to reclaim. Also, in very few instances, land was awarded. The Taos Pueblo in New Mexico won a suit to regain use of Blue Lake. The Yakima tribe received 21,000 acres in central Washington (New York Times Index).

Even though there appeared to be some initiatives on the part of the federal government to reform, AIM continued to encourage the escalation of protests. In the summer of 1972, a major march, the "Trail of Broken Treaties," was formed by AIM activists. This demonstration started in California and ended in Washington, D.C. Five hundred people participated. For six days, activists occupied the BIA building, demanding amnesty and a return to tribal sovereignty. One week later, federal authorities gave the protesters immunity from prosecution and funds to help the marchers return home, but little else (Weyler 1982).

This event, unfortunately, did little to increase tribal sovereignty. It did, however, get the attention of the media and as a result sparked other protests. In support of the BIA occupation, 50 Indians invaded the BIA office in Custer, S.D., and initiated a sit-in. In another event, AIM organized a protest in Nebraska, where 200 Indians clashed with police, seeking a stiffer sentence for a white man who had killed an Indian. The courthouse was burned, 8 Indians injured, and 36 AIM members arrested. Another incident in Rapid City, S.D., was held in support of those demonstrating against the light sentence. Twenty Indians were injured and 40 arrested.

From February 27, 1973, through May 8, 1973, under the leadership of AIM, the town of Wounded Knee on Pine Ridge Reservation in South Dakota was occupied. This action made it inevitable that a qualitatively higher stage of resistance had developed. The site of this large occupation was symbolic to many Native Americans. This is the site where the infamous December 29, 1890, Wounded Knee massacre occurred. After the army disarmed Sioux warriors, the soldiers opened fire, killing an estimated 300 Indians, mostly women and children.

In the occupation of February 1973, AIM demanded that the government investigate BIA practices on all Sioux Reservations in South Dakota, that the government recognize the 1868 Fort Laramie Treaty, which formally gave Sioux sovereignty over much of what is now the Dakotas, Montana, Wyoming, and Nebraska, and eliminate federal control over Indians. An AIM founder and chair, Vernon Bellecourt, said, "the group organized the 1973 Wounded Knee occupation to draw maximum attention to the plight of American Indians" (Bellecourt Interview, 1986). Law enforcement officials, the military, and the FBI surrounded the occupiers. The confrontation ended in a negotiated settlement, albeit more symbolic than substantial. With all of the media coverage, there is little doubt that most Americans now understood the plight of Indians. They may not have agreed with it, but they now knew about it—ignorance could not be claimed.

In the following table, general movement activities are recorded. Data from 1960 to 1983, collected from the New York Times Index, illustrates a rise and decline in movement activities. In the end, more than 100 Indians were arrested, two were killed, and 15 injured. Wounded Knee clearly illustrates the repressive nature of the government. The Nixon Administration responded as if it was a war rather than a peaceful occupation. Nixon ordered that "troops, tanks, planes and helicopters" go to Wounded Knee "to teach the Indian militants a lesson" (Ortiz 1984, 160).

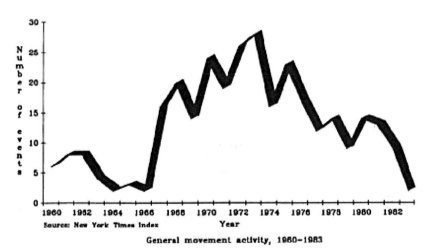

General movement activity, 1960–1983

The effect Wounded Knee had on the movement and on society in general was enormous. This event sparked a number of events across the nation. Indians and non-Indians in support of Indian grievances and in support of the occupiers of Wounded Knee staged many events. However, the federal government attempted to suppress this support as well. For example, federal authorities intercepted a caravan representing "people of all races" when they attempted to bring food for the militants at Wounded Knee. A group of Chippewa and Iroquois were charged with intent to incite a riot when they crossed the state line in support of the Wounded Knee occupiers. In addition, while transporting supplies to Wounded Knee, 13 supporters were arrested on charges of violating federal antiriot laws.

Although the Occupation of Alcatraz in 1969, the Trail of Broken Treaties caravan in 1972, and the Occupation of Wounded Knee in 1973 were the most dramatic and most publicized events of American Indians, many other events occurred. A 100-mile march took place in Raleigh, North Carolina, in support of Indians controlling Indian schools. Twenty Indians and Black supporters were arrested for protesting on the steps of the North Carolina State Indian Commission building when they sought to gain recognition as members of the Tuscarora Tribe. In Sacramento, California, six armed Indians were arrested after they occupied the site of a proposed governor's mansion that occupiers claim was an ancient burial ground. In the Black Hills in South Dakota, over 500 Indians occupied the area, stating the land is Indian land. In addition, in February of 1978, AIM member Clyde Bellecourt led more than 200 Native Americans on the "Longest Walk" from Alcatraz to Washington, D.C. to protest a rash of anti-Indian legislation.

With AIM still at the organizational helm, conventional tactics were seen as basically ineffective. Courts continued being used, but not as widely. The number of positive responses by the government to the demands of Indians began to decline significantly, and they were still activities that dealt with less volatile issues; they dealt mainly with civil rights—the right to segregated schools, the use of peyote in religious rites—and less with land and money matters. Furthermore, for the first time in contemporary society, land was taken away under the guise of serving larger society, primarily for national parks.

More importantly, this period reflects heavy government repression in almost all of the protests that followed. Many arrests, injuries, and some deaths occurred. During the year following Wounded Knee, over 300 Indian deaths occurred at the hands of police and federal authorities. Between 1970 and 1976, hundreds, perhaps thousands, of Black and Indian activists, particularly the leadership, were murdered or imprisoned. While many activists of all protesting groups felt heavy repression, "the attacks on Indian demonstrators and organizers and especially AIM activists were particularly brutal, with a far greater ration of deaths and imprisonments than any other sector" (Ortiz 1984a, 167).

AFTER THE PEAK

After the Occupation of Wounded Knee and through 1978, the number of protests declined significantly. Moreover, while the number of protesters at a single event did not drastically change, the length of the protest declined. It became obvious that the government would not tolerate another lengthy occupation. Furthermore, many of these events resulted in the deaths or incarceration of AIM leaders and/or protesters (Means interview 1988).

One of the reasons speculated for the increased government suppression is that the government had already experienced the tumultuous '60s. During this period, local and federal troops mobilized to suppress Blacks, Chicanos, students, and whites. The response of the government to Native protest may have been a response to societal upheaval in general. A speedy roundup of the "troublemakers" may have been a signal from the U.S. Government that protest of any kind would not be tolerated. Government did not suppress organizations such as the NCAI that provided funds for voting rights, and the Native American Rights Funds, a national Indian interest law firm (Echohawk interview 1988). Marches and other forms of civil disobedience became acceptable forms of strategies for native activists.

Subsequently, the basic complexion of the Native American movement changed markedly, partially because of the increased suppression of Indians and partially because non-Indian supporters saw Wounded Knee as a government fiasco. As a result, membership in AIM and other Indian organizations changed. The movement began to attract an increase in non-Indian supporters, including environmentalists and those individuals concerned with religious and cultural rights (Gurwitz Interview 1986).

Furthermore, since AIM's hegemony over the movement's formal organizational structure was decreasing, other less militant groups developed. None of these organizations, however, succeeded in dominating the movement's formal structure, as AIM had been able to do earlier.

The relative calm prevailing on most reservations since the late 1970s does not necessarily suggest that Native Americans are less actively committed to the goals they once held so fervently. On the contrary, the movement changed in order to accommodate the political climate of the time. Purged of many of its more radical leaders after Wounded Knee, and thus leaving few Indians who were able to generate enthusiasm, and fewer who were willing to take risks, the movement had no choice but to change. In addition, the movement was infiltrated heavily by the FBI. Consequently, a United Nations committee investigated FBI agents. While this did little to curtail government actions, it did contribute heavily to the reluctance of protesters to challenge the government in the same militant way. Consequently, many activists began to work on local issues that pertained to their particular environment, and less with national issues. In addition, a number of Indians joined the efforts of non-Indian organizations, specifically those that focused on environmental issues and religious freedom. Many Indians began to view these organizations as the vehicle for change.

However, activism within the United States did not completely disappear. Such events as the fight against the relocation of Navajos in Arizona, and the dispute between the Mohawks and the governments of Canada and the United States support this statement. It also illustrates that activism in the domestic arena changed markedly in the absence of a centralized organizational structure such as AIM.

Because of Wounded Knee and the subsequent actions of the government, many activists realized how instrumental the federal government was in blocking their progress toward self-determination. New methods of achieving their goals needed to be initiated.

A NEW KIND OF ACTIVISM

Marginalized groups, like American Indians, have historically used social movement activity as a strategy to generate power and social change. In the late 1950s and 1960s, litigation was used by a number of protesting groups with some success. The most notable of these was the work of the litigation activities of the early Civil Rights Movement regarding issues of school desegregation. Federal courts were more willing to open their doors to the claims of the disenfranchised and certain minority groups in American society. The Warren Court, particularly, provided a period of judicial activism unforeseen in earlier periods. The apparent success in civil rights litigation and the receptivity of courts encouraged other groups to adopt litigation as a strategy.

Similar to activists in the Civil Rights Movement, American Indian activists advocated law reform in their efforts to seek greater tribal self-determination. Given Indians' relationship with federal and state governments and the administrative machinery (BIA) created to control them, it has been difficult to increase the rights of Indians within typical mainstream politics such as those strictly associated with institutional methods.

Indian activists resurfaced in the early 1990s with new leaders and new ideas on how to generate social change. During this time, Indian activism shifted from the cities and more directly to federally recognized reservations, from the streets into the courtrooms, and once again began demanding a level of tribal sovereignty. Land and culture continued to be key issues, but sovereignty in economic development became major goals as well.

For most movements, as long as the tactics are nonviolent, society and public officials accord them greater legality and legitimacy. Therefore, the use of courts for Indians has made their issues more salient and led to greater responses by the federal government than have other forms of collective behavior, certainly more than those tactics that encompass the use of violence.

In 1986, congressional leaders initiated the Indian Gaming Regulatory Act (IGRA) that essentially stated tribal governments could initiate gaming but were encouraged to go into a compact (agreement of some sort) with states contributing to less conflict. States interpret the IGRA as unfair and suggest it gives tribes too much power. Powerful corporate casino owners continue to fuel the animosity toward Indians by suggesting Indians receive preferential treatment. High-powered constituents voice their fear of organized crime that often follows gambling. States assert the IGRA violates the 10th and 11th Amendments. Indians confront and debate with each other as to the consequences of this relatively new form of economic development. In addition, among all of these various actors and diverse interests, tribes push ahead with their inherent rights of tribal sovereignty, historically limited but certainly not given to them by the federal government. Here are the conditions for increased Indian political activity and the increased use of litigation as a tool for social reform. It is within this context that Indians are increasingly becoming political actors.

For the first time, the battle over Indian gaming forced tribal governments to hire high-priced Washington lobbying firms to appeal to Congress in an attempt to make the system Indians confront less adversary. For example, the Viejas Tribe of Alpine, California, and the Cabazon Band of Mission Indians of Indio, California, hired the Jefferson Group, a major Washington public affairs group that represented the tribes on a number of issues besides gaming.

The use of lobbying as a strategy points to the realization on the part of tribal governments that politics have clearly taken a major shift from protest in the streets to the hallways of Congress and eventually to the courts. As the resources of tribal governments increase and as they become familiar with how American politics is played, the level of tribal sovereignty has increased. The second largest casino in the world, the Foxwoods Casino in Connecticut, run by the tiny Mashantucket Pequot Tribe, grossed approximately $600 million dollars in 1993. Tribes have been able to build schools, community centers, child-development centers, and new housing, and provide college tuition and health care because of this new political resource.

Consequently, the type of activities Indians use has been and will continue to be a strange mixture of institutional and noninstitutional strategies. Various tribal rights are at the heart of Indian sovereignty and continue to play a role in Indian activism. If we mix in with sovereignty, levels of self-determination, tribal federal recognition, state jurisdiction, intertribal conflict, and stir in the free market, notably corporate interests, and states seeking to increase their jurisdiction and protect their citizens, we have an arena of increased conflict ready to explode on any given day.

Indian mobilization is largely shaped by the political and economic context within which Indians live. The formation of Indian activists is a response to a structure largely determined by federal Indian policies, i.e., Congress. Indian activism is a tactical reaction to policies that Indians believe to be unfair.

The diverse interests, therefore, will generate a new kind of Indian activism, one that will continue to be fought in the courtroom. The shift to the courtroom does not suggest that the protest on reservations will cease, however. Like the 1970s, the activists of the 1990s and the new millennium realize pressure must be maintained against certain interests within the reservation, while their lawyers battle it out in the halls of justice. Given the confusion, ambiguity, and self-interest of Congress, litigation will undoubtedly be the preferred strategy in issues regarding tribal sovereignty.

Like other disenfranchised, excluded, and disillusioned Americans, Indians designed an explosive movement, one that to many Indians generated pride in their heritage, if nothing more. Nevertheless, the government could not allow disruptive politics to become the norm as it seemed it had because of the tumultuous '60s. The U.S. Government stopped the movement quickly and funneled that disruptive anger into more institutional means.

Interestingly enough, the Domestic Dependent status, created by Chief Justice Marshall in 1830, provides tribal governments with a powerful legal tool that other protesting groups do not have. This is a political relationship, not a racial one, and is based on the inherent sovereignty of tribal governments. The unique status of tribal governments no doubt makes them more vulnerable not only to interests outside of their territory but also to interests within their territory by their respective members. Two examples provided earlier, Martinez v. Santa Clara Pueblo Nation and Native American Church v. Navajo Tribal Council, demonstrate the type of pressure members can apply on tribal governments. When its members, as in the above cases, challenge tribal sovereignty, the highest courts often uphold the doctrine of tribal sovereignty. In other situations, Indians may have to organize and challenge tribal and federal power. For example, American Indian women must fight not only racial and cultural oppression off the reservations, but also face the realities of discrimination on the reservation; their plight is discussed in the following chapter.

QUESTIONS FOR DISCUSSION:

1) What is the main focus of the American Indian Movement? How can it be said that without AIM there would not have been subsequent legislation that favored Indians?
2) How are tribal governments able to use the courts to get their needs met?
3) Explain the iron triangle as it pertains to Indian interests?
4) To what extent can one say the activities of AIM were successful?
5) Identify the main characteristics of institutional and noninstitutional tactics?

CHAPTER EIGHT

INDIGENOUS WOMEN

We got those changes for them, and that's what the chiefs never realized—we're on their side. We've always been for Native rights and the good of all Native people, the First Nations. The time has come for men to stop fighting against the women and start listening to us and working with us (Silman 1987, 15).

In Martinez v. Santa Clara Pueblo Nation, 1978, the Supreme Court agreed with the tribe's argument that tribal membership is a matter for the tribe to determine, not the federal government. Consequently, the child of Julia Martinez could not be enrolled in either tribe of the parent even though she is a full-blooded Indian. Martinez, a member of the Santa Clara Pueblo, sued her tribe because it did not recognize her daughter as a member. Santa Clara Pueblo consider children of male tribal members eligible for membership, but children of female members who marry nonmembers, as Ms. Martiniz did, are ineligible. Unlike many other Indian nations, the Santa Clara Pueblo is a patrilineal society, where membership is defined through the father. Since the father of the child is not a member of the Santa Clara Pueblo, the child could not be tribally enrolled in the Santa Clara Pueblo Nation.

When tribal members similar to the above case challenge tribal sovereignty, the Supreme Court often upholds the doctrine of tribal sovereignty. If the issue is an economic issue, as in the *Lyng v. Northwest Indian Cemetery Protective Association* discussed in previous chapters, tribal sovereignty is usually not upheld. As Justice O'Connor stated, economic rights outweigh religious rights of Indians. She could have just stated that economic rights outweigh all rights of Indians, because the recent decisions of the Supreme Court demonstrate this.

In order to stop legislated sexual discrimination of Native women, tribal members are often forced to organize and challenge tribal or federal power, as in the case of the Tobique women in Canada. In June of 1985, the Canadian Parliament passed a bill that would allow the Tobique Reserve women in New Brunswick, Canada, the right to be defined as members of their tribe. The new bill amended the original Indian Act that deprived women of receiving assistance to which they were normally entitled. Similar to the Santa Clara Pueblo Nation, the original Indian Act was based on a patrilineal system, a system where a person's tribal status was determined by a person's relationship to a male, who is a direct descendant in the male line of another male. Subsequently, when a Canadian Indian woman married a nonstatus man, known as "marrying out," she lost her Indian status and was unable to regain it. In contrast, the wife and children of an Indian man received his status, even if they were nonnative. This made a Canadian Indian woman virtually dependent upon father and husband for her identity, rights, and status (Silman 1987).

Whether or not the Pueblo Nation and the Maliseets (Tobique) are traditionally patrilineal is irrelevant. Native women in matrilineal nations share similar experiences. Imposed patriarchal structures have the wherewithal to withstand any number of events, situations, and desire for change, demonstrating that the consequences of colonization run deep. Furthermore, any attempts by women to change gender bias laws are rarely supported by tribal leaders. Many of the Canadian Native women who supported the amendment process of the Indian Act were attacked by Indian leaders, labeled as "whitewashed women's libbers" undermining their Indian heritage, stated Canadian Native women who supported the amendment process of the Indian Act. Similarly, efforts by Martinez to appeal the court's decision would have been defined by tribal members as challenging tribal sovereignty, making it difficult, if not impossible, for her to pursue her self-interest.

Moreover, Native women in both countries who challenge tribal sovereignty are often accused of tampering with the special legal status held by both Native populations. Fear of a return to the Termination Era of the 1950s is cited as a reason not to support women's rights.

No doubt, all Native people remain cognizant of termination. However, within larger society and in Indian society, women's issues are often viewed as "women's work," not the work of the tribe. We know all too well that women's issues tend to go largely ignored specifically in racial or ethnic groups where racism, or in the case of Native people, colonization, is viewed as the more cogent issue. In fact, women who work on women's issues rather than the defined interest of the group are viewed as selfish and self-centered and identified by members of the group as not being of that group. In other cases, these women are identified as "too European."

In the liberation struggles of the American indigenous peoples, it is no different. Women of color, states Jaimes-Guerrero, "generally tend not to favor the notion of "politics" which would divide and weaken their communities by defining "male energy as the enemy.""

Narrow interpretations of feminism, Marxism and other "isms" are often rejected purely on the notion that they are Eurocentric, that they come from progressive non-Indian nations and the US. Government, where "divide and conquer" tactics have been practiced. Therefore, it is not surprising that Indians would be highly suspicious of anything with a tinge of whiteness to it and interpret these doctrines as continuing colonization in the name of "gender equity." "We are American Indian women, in that order," stated Lorelei Deora Means, one of the founders of Women of All Red Nations (WARN) (Jaimes and Halsey 1992, 331–336). While WARN was an indigenous women's organization, it was oppression, specifically colonization, that they were fighting, not gender inequality.

History suggests that the disempowerment of Indian women corresponds closely with colonial domination. However, there is little to suggest that with decolonization, native women would once again become empowered. The imposed tribal governments transformed indigenous male attitudes toward women, and continued the process of imperialism begun by consolidating patriarchal and racist gender values into tribal structures. Even in those tribal governments where women have become tribal leaders, American Indian men continue to be the chief beneficiary, not women.

Incidents of inequality of Indian women have a history and a chronology to them that is traceable. Colonization occurred within a people that has been neither completely conquered nor completely assimilated. Had assimilation of American Indian women been complete, we would have to examine racism and sexism as it applies in American society and institutions, possibly thus giving the typical feminist approach more usefulness and increased validity. As it is, most of the inequality of Indian women is rooted in federal government policies and events. Removal and relocation polices thrust various and culturally different tribes together, forcing new and sometimes different divisions among men and women. Failed assimilation policies like the General Allotment Act and Urban relocation attempted to change the historical power Indian women possessed and their control over land. Euro-Americans imposed racial hierarchy and its gender politics on tribal government through the Indian Reorganization Act that further disempowered women from politics. The indoctrination of Indian men into the all-male administrative machinery, specifically the BIA, secured economic rights for men while eroding rights for women. Insidious paternalistic Christian religions and white educational systems that focused on domesticating women diminished the rights of women. Some contemporary legislation created to provide self-determination for the tribe and increased rights for women may in reality be more illusionary than establishing any meaningful level of self-determination.

These structural entities combined with gender socialization and situational constraints have firmly set the stage for the increased inequality of women on and off the reservation. However, the process of gender-related inequality and violence began during the high level of colonial penetration by Europeans. This process was continued and maintained by the creation of federal Indian legislation developed to meet the needs of the *new* Americans, not the *first* Americans. In order for this process to take hold, Indigenous men were forced to perpetuate the same type of gender inequality that was practiced by the new Americans. Consequently, indigenous women were displaced from their indigenous purpose, and relegated to an unfamiliar, inferior, and often subjugated position to Indian men and to whites.

While some colonizers, specifically the French and Spanish, may have had less aversion to interracial unions and may have treated Indian women somewhat differently than the English, there is little to suggest they were more equal or less oppressive. All colonizers drew upon their own histories and experiences in their treatment of American Indian women. What can be gleaned from these histories is that women within Europe were often viewed as being "no worse than domesticated animals" (Mama 1997).

Bringing these ideas with them, the English arrived eager to create a new and free nation full of liberties and equality, albeit with the exclusion and participation of women. For sure, it would have been impossible to create the kind of nation the English envisioned had Native women participated in politics at the same level they had prior to the arrival of the Europeans, largely because at this time the new American government was giving shape to developing its racist ideologies and practices. The new Americans believed the economic and political development of the United States was dependent upon the transformation of both Indian men and women in the way they organized, socialized, and politicized. Consequently, in their pursuit of capitalist models of development, the new Americans created a system of gender inequality within larger society and within Indian communities.

In no other period was this transformation apparent as in the fur trade of the eastern interior of North America. During this early period, Indians were incorporated into a mercantile economy dominated by a few European states. The purpose of this relationship was to make Indians producers of fur and consumers of European products. Incorporation into the labor force, the first and last of its type, significantly transformed the gender division of labor that had for many years sustained the livelihood of Indians. Indian men were forced to hunt for more and more furs, while Indian women tended to fiercely defend and maintain their traditions, culture, lifestyle, and equality, an equality that would prove to be an impediment to the envisioned economic development of the Europeans.

Since Indian women were seen by the early Euro-Americans as wielding power over Indian men, it was important to transform the Indian man to take charge of "his woman," similarly to European men. Confining women to the home, defined as domesticating women, was a precondition for the transfer of power from women to men, and in the end made it easier for Europeans to create male-dominated structures and systems.

Not much changed with the decline of the fur trade. Europeans continued in their attempts to solve their dilemma of acquiring Indian land; land that traditionally was in the hands of Indian women. The "Indian problem," as seen by Euro-Americans and defined by Stephen Cornell in his book *The Return of the Native,* was an economic problem, that is, how best to get the Indian's land without Indians knowing and reacting to it. For the first three centuries from 1600 to 1800, Europeans, and subsequently the U.S. Government, developed treaties and then policy after policy in their attempt to solve this problem. Naturally, the focus on domesticating Indian women became primary, specifically since women were the caretakers and holders of the land. By the removal period in the 1830s, male tribal leaders began to adopt nontribal ideas as they related to the role of women. American Indian men experienced increased benefits by conforming to and participating in these ideas even though, as demonstrated below, American Indian men did not approve of the manner in which white men treated white women. Indian men often thought the laws of whites showed they cared little for their women, and that all they wanted women for was to work the land. (Wagner 2001.)

Cornell states that although Indian communities were severely transformed, the new American still needed to culturally transform Indian women, because as land changed from the hands of Indians to whites, Indian women experienced less equality. Furthermore, women were socialized to become subservient not only to whites but to Indian men as well. By all accounts, this did not occur at any high rate. If anything, the displacement of women from the land through the Indian Removal Act and the General Allotment Act contributed to high levels of hunger among Indians. Women were no longer able to cultivate the land as they had traditionally done. This period marked the beginning of converting the role of Indian women from the land to the home. Americans hoped that with the transfer of land from women to men, the transfer of power out of the hands of women and into the hands of men would follow. This would alter the way tribes organized and interacted with the federal government and begin to solve the second Indian problem: cultural transformation, attempts to transform Indians ranging from total exclusion to annihilation.

Given the historical consequences of dominant society on the various Indian cultures, how then was gender inequality to be reversed? Efforts by women and men to reverse many of the consequences of colonization would need to be developed by Indian men and women, for colonizers are not known for liberating the colonized. Today, some Indian women suggest American Indian women do not need liberation. They suggest that they have always been liberated within their tribal structure. This is somewhat correct. The previous historical account supports this. However, to suggest that liberation is not needed is to maintain tribal structures were not manipulated, transformed, and controlled by the American federal government. It is also to suggest that the campaign to remove, relocate, (adopt, board-out, foster-out, farm-out) and assimilate many Indians had little to no consequences. On the contrary, many Indian women believe they still need to liberate themselves from the consequences of capitalism, civilization, and Christianization. This liberation would in essence require a separate process of decolonization, one that will challenge the sexism created on tribal grounds by the federal government.

It is unfair and incorrect to suggest that American Indian communities and nations are free of gender abuse and inequality merely because they are geographically separated from larger society or because of cultural traditions closely tied to matrilineal and matriarchy, two explanations often provided. These explanations tend to suggest that American Indian cultures are stagnant, thereby overlooking the impact of patriarchal civilization. History has taken its toll on Indians and disproportionately on Indian women and their land. The transfer of land out of the hands of Indian women contributed to the pollution of water and land, the destruction of land, disruption of the ecosystems, and inappropriate land-use patterns. Since many problems faced by the global arena today are traced to the treatment and use of land, traditional Indians believe that had women been left as the caretakers of the land, fewer of these problems would exist. More specifically, without the subjugation of American Indian women and men, it is unlikely that the United States would have developed such a strong economic, social, and political base. To be sure, economic growth was dependent upon acquisition of Indian land. Additionally, the acquisition of liberty and equality and property for the new Americans was dependent upon stripping Indians of theirs.

This raises the question as to whether American Indian women experienced greater liberation with the demise of colonial rule and the creation of tribal governments governed by Indians. Would Indian nationalists, largely men, merely continue the trajectories of contempt and disempowerment, as has been shown to be the case in other nationalist movements? Given the time and effort put into changing the relations between Indian men and women plus the natural tendency of nationalist movements, it is unlikely that men would further work to restore gender equality. There is also little evidence to suggest that indigenous elites, historically men, would revert to more traditional ways regarding women. On the contrary, there is much evidence to suggest the opposite.

Given this reality, what are the options of Indian women?

A major criticism of Marxism or feminism is that they are Eurocentric paradigms. Does this then mean that we should automatically disregard their validity in providing some usefulness in the struggle of Native women for equality? To suggest that these paradigms are "being perpetuated at the expense of the indigenous worldview" is narrow and misleading. In reality, the campaign against feminism and Marxism has occurred at the expense of forming any critical analysis of gender socialization within Indian communities. That is to say, it is easier to criticize the federal government, Marxism, and white women, good straw men and easy targets, than it is to develop a critical analysis about native men and women. We now know that many of the women in the civil rights movements did not examine the dichotomies at play between men and women within that movement until the movement was well over. Indian women, largely Indian activists, have not developed a critical analysis of men in the American Indian Movement either. Consequently, the power and abuse of power by men in powerful positions within the tribal structure, the community or the movement, has largely gone unchallenged. In many cases, what holds Indian women back from examining their situation is an assumption held by many minority women: the assumption that, somehow, women of color are exempt from patriarchy; that Indian cultures are free of domination; and that Indian men are not dominating. To hold colonization solely responsible without forming a more contemporary explanation tied to colonization does little to change the pattern of abuse and inequality, or reverse its tendencies. Until American Indian women and men can face the reality that sexism empowers men despite the overall impact of colonialism, it will be difficult to engage in any meaningful dialog about gender. In addition, until all women can face the reality that women cannot achieve real equality under the strategies and tactics of neoliberal, patriarchal politics, little will change.

Therefore, what might be useful is realizing that the sense of priorities of Indian women are radically and irrevocably different from those espoused by the mainstream women's movement. First, Indian women were not integrated into the economic structure portraying different types and levels of subjugation and oppression as African, Asian, and Latin women. The gender division of labor for Indian women was not illuminated through sexual work, factory work, domestic work, or informal work. Consequently, the limited integration of Indians into the economic structure, the level of wage inequality experienced by native women, is significantly smaller and different when compared with other women. This may be one reason why liberal feminist ideas geared toward pay equity and equality do not resonate well among Indian women. As Piven and Cloward (1978, 23) suggest, "people cannot defy institutions to which they have no access, and to which they make no contribution."

Still, it was the incorporation of men into the fur trade, and subsequently into other forms of economic development that changed the lives of Indian women. Within the economy there is no direct consequence to Indian women. However, since one of the traits of traditional societies is collective, any effort to move toward an individual lifestyle, significantly disrupts the collective as a whole.

The search for an understanding of the sources and nature of Native women's oppression and for an appropriate remedy for it, may well serve as the basis for analyzing the usefulness of any one of the strands of feminism. Whether we examine and integrate portions of the liberal equal rights version of feminism, radical feminism that is deeply rooted in male dominance, or socialist feminism, which views the oppression of women as a part of the workings of capitalism is irrelevant. To have a narrow interpretation of feminist theories or disregard their importance may not increase the equality of Native women.

Clearly, Indian women must fight not only gender oppression but also racial and cultural oppression. Indian women who live off reservations, consisting of about two-thirds of the native population, and on the reservation must face the realities of sexism, racism, and colonization off reservation. When they return to the reservation, they face sexism, sexual abuse, and colonization. Therefore, the different manifestations of sexism and violence on the reservations should not, nonetheless, be trivialized, ignored, or not recognized as gender related even though the larger issue of tribal sovereignty reigns.

By focusing on change from the bottom up and attacking elite—indigenous and nonindigenous—structures and systems, the Tobique women in Canada were able to expand their rights. The Canadian women first accepted the realities and consequences of their history and organized a movement where that history did not overshadow their main goal of gender equality. This is a classic case where tribal sovereignty was working against the interests of women. The organizers of this movement first realized and identified the patterns of subjugation, that is, sexual discrimination, and shaped their resistance accordingly, moving from *hopeless submission to hopeful noncompliance.*

The Tobique women shared their testimony about their conditions, but not without high risks. The Indian Act that governed the life of Indians and defined who is and who is not legally Indian was finally amended. A portion of the Act, mainly the part that stripped women of their rights if they married non-status men, was earmarked for change. As early as 1970, Native women began to organize across Canada, as stated in the following:

> We Mohawk women were the first to complain about Indian women losing our birthright. When the Tobique women came along and joined the fight, we were delighted. I was honored to be with them when they started the march to Ottawa that triggered publicity about Indian women fights for rights. With their continued help we hope all our Native sisters will be able to go home to their people in peace (Silman 1987, 247).

By 1977, the United Nations had agreed to hear their case on the grounds that Native women had no legal recourse left in Canada. From 1977 until 1981, when the U.N. Human Rights Committee ruled in favor of finding Canada in breach of the International Covenant on Civil and Political Rights, the Tobique women held long walks and numerous events all in an effort to bring attention to their cause.

In the end, the efforts of the Tobique women changed the Act and increased Indian sovereignty even though the men did not see it that way. Structurally, Indian men had acquired all of the political resources and lobbying power to obstruct the women's efforts, and certainly did not view it as furthering tribal sovereignty. To the contrary, they viewed this change as if they were losing power. Because of the women's work, Indian Affairs of Canada allowed Indian people to decide their membership rather than that decision being made from the top-down as it had been done historically.

As the Tobique women demonstrated, working outside of the tribal structure for change had more potential of furthering Indian sovereignty than did working within the confines of the existing sexist tribal structure. That is to say, in their efforts to achieve gender equality, the consciousness of male tribal leaders and of all Indians was heavily affected, leading to an increase in tribal sovereignty rather than a decrease as presupposed.

American Indian women have a similar historical experience of other indigenous women and those women of color who came before Indians in examining gender roles in their communities. Therefore, we should not suggest that the so-called white (privileged-class)-feminists contribute nothing to the plight of women of color. To the contrary, American Indian women will eventually develop a feminist theory that specifically addresses sexism, racism, and colonization, a theory that is able to fight on many fronts, while maintaining a set of principles built on politics of self-determination rather than politics of inclusion. That is to say, women of *all* colors must pay special attention to their particular patterns of subjugation, for it is within these patterns that lay the various shapes of their resistance.

Historically, Indian women have demonstrated a willingness to defer rather than forgo their personal interest, suggesting their focus continues to remain on the interest of the whole. However, it is the cumulative impact of deferring that has the potential of leading to a loss of collective interest. Tobique women did not allow this to happen. They organized and worked on their interests that proved to be in the interests of the collective. While tactics are prone to create change—whether targeting sexist federal legislation, corrupt tribal government, or abusive Indian men—the goal remains the same: gender equality translates into greater tribal sovereignty as the Tobique women demonstrated.

Gender inequality and violence of indigenous women began during the high level of European colonial penetration; federal Indian legislation sustained this process. In order for this process to take hold, indigenous men perpetuated the same type of gender inequality that was practiced by the new Americans. Consequently, indigenous women were displaced from their indigenous purpose and relegated to an unfamiliar, inferior, and subjugated position. Because of this treatment, the relationship between American Indian men and women changed dramatically, contributing to a higher level of conflict and gender inequality within and outside of tribal governments.

THE VIOLENCE AGAINST WOMEN ACT, 2013

A good start toward increasing gender equality on Indian nations might be to recognize that Native American women experience the highest rate of violence of any group in the United States. A report released by the Department of Justice, American Indians and Crime, found that Native American women suffer violent crime at a rate three and a half times higher than the national average. Researchers estimate that this rate is actually much higher since over 70% of sexual assaults, according to the Department of Justice, are never reported.

In addition to domestic abuse, Native women also experience the highest levels of sexual and domestic abuse of any group. A report from the American Indian Women's Chemical Health Project found that three-fourths of Native women have experienced some type of sexual assault in their lives. These abuses go unreported largely because Native women know the history of tribal agencies in prosecuting these crimes, and largely because of lack of resources and lack of jurisdiction. Police and courts tend to ignore cases of violence involving Native women owing to alleged confusion between federal and tribal jurisdiction. As was shown in an earlier chapter, any cases involving non-Native and Native automatically fall under federal jurisdiction. Moreover, since 70% or more of violence experienced by Native women is committed by persons not of the same race, (and certainly not of the same tribe), law enforcement and attorneys chose to ignore these cases. Low resources are often the excuse. But many Indian people see their issues as a very low priority.

In a hearing on the Violence Against Women's Act 2012, there was opposition to protect LGBT people, Native American women, and undocumented immigrants for various reasons. Representative Gwen Moore (D-Wes.) said that Republicans' opposition to include the three groups above runs counter to the act "being called *Violence Against Women* if you don't protect all women." When it came to Native American women, one recommendation was to give tribal courts increased authority to prosecute incidents committed by non-Natives in Native territories.

Few of us thought this recommendation would be accepted. However, in 2013, the Violence Against Women Act was expanded to allow Native nations to prosecute non-Indians in cases involving domestic violence. The Pascua Yaqui tribe in Arizona is the first tribe set to prosecute the first non-Indian under the new law. Some members of Congress raised concerns about the capacity of non-Indians receiving a fair trial by a group of Indian jurors. What is interesting about their concern is that there have never been any concerns raised about Indians receiving a fair trial by non-Indian jurors.

Nonetheless, this is a step in the right direction to increasing tribal sovereignty and increasing the rights of Native women. It is hoped that issues between tribal governments and the rights of Native women will be sorted out more equally as well. Certainly, as Native women become tribal presidents and continue to be included on tribal governments, change is bound to occur.

QUESTIONS FOR DISCUSSION:

1) Explain how the transformation of Indian women corresponds with colonial domination.

2) How were the Tobique women able to reverse the Indian Act?

3) To what extent does greater gender equality translate into greater tribal sovereignty?

4) Define matrilineal and patrilineal. How do these terms explain and shape the behavior of traditional Indians?

5) How does the Violence Against Women Act have the capacity of increasing Native women rights and tribal sovereignty?

CHAPTER NINE

SURVIVAL OF TRIBAL GOVERNMENTS

What is the goal of any nation it if is not self-determination? (Cook-Lynn 2007, 210).

Many native scholars and native people agree and suggest that not many more years will pass before tribal governments have the political mastery necessary to achieve true sovereignty and complete self-government. As complicated as tribal governments are, there are important positive changes that have occurred, either because of time, increased government support, or because tribal governments have learned to assert themselves. Some tribal governments have created a system that complements the old and the new, the traditional and the modern, while staying cognizant of federal government and its administrative machinery, the BIA. The age of self-determination starting in the 1970s provided tribes with some opportunities to undertake activities that were more aligned with tribal interests. Still, in most cases, the BIA and the federal government continue to be an irritant rather than a benefit.

Historically, a nation's power is determined by the size of its territory, its population, its level of autonomy, national resources, and, among other things, its level of economic power. To measure the power of Indian nations, however, we must pay special attention to its leadership and the capacity of this leadership to meet the needs of its citizenship and assert its self-determination. In most Indian nations, the power of its citizens compared with the power of its tribal political elites seems to be fluctuating in favor of its citizens. That is to say, Indian nations are slowly becoming a tool of its members rather than strictly a tool of the federal government. This shift is occurring as Indians assert themselves into tribal politics rather than shunning it, thus minimizing the control of federally appointed indigenous elites who governed in the past with little legitimate authority. To maintain and then sustain their legitimacy, tribal managers are forced to share the few rewards of tribal policies with all of their citizens rather than keep it for themselves and their immediate families, as was done by Tribal Chief Dick Wilson of Pine Ridge Reservation. In addition, the pro-gaming activities have given some tribes the possibility of increasing their ability to self-govern while managing tribal–state conflict.

Regardless of the issue, whether gaming, water rights, fishing rights, land claim rights or treaty violations, or tribal sovereignty, tribal governments continue to demand that the federal government relax if not relinquish its paternalistic power over them largely because its members are making those demands. Naturally, some tribal governments have been more successful than others, and much of that success can be attributed to the political skills they have gained. The survival of tribal governments, therefore, is highly dependent upon the historical dance that unfolded between Indians, whites, and the federal government, and to what extent Indian nations demand that they be the ones to create Indian legislation. Historically, federal Indian legislation was created with little to no Indian participation. This resulted in policies benefiting whites, not Indians. Recently, however, tribal governments have been able to sway Indian legislation in its favor. Let us examine one important piece of legislation, the Native American Grave Protection and Repatriation Act (NAGPRA) 1991.

Even though numerous scientists, archaeologists, and museums disagreed with its passage, it did pass. In a Denver newspaper article in December 1996, editorialist Philip Terzian states that the NAGPRA is an example of "the lunacy of federal Indian policy." Terzian wrote that not to allow scientists' access to a 10,000-year-old site to analyze human remains was a pattern of "scientific vandalism repeated many times since enactment of the (act), threatening research and museum acquisitions." This is somewhat true. The act was implemented to stop the vandalism of sacred sites that has been repeated many times since the arrival of the Europeans, and was passed to stop museums from taking the remains of Indians and displaying them. By allowing Indians, not whites, the right to define a site as sacred, Indian have a religious and spiritual reverence for the remains of their ancestors. This is not much different than what many people from every culture demands. It is speculative to say that Terzian would not want anyone digging up the remains of his ancestors and putting them on display in museums. However, Terzian's article demonstrates the inability of Euro-Americans to understand the main tenets of land-based religions and the cultural connection Indigenous peoples have to the earth and everything in it.

Terzian wraps up his argument in the old adage: "Indians are not the original inhabitants of this continent, so what rights do they have?" Americans will continue to debate where American aborigines "came from" (if indeed they came from somewhere else) in the same way they debate evolution and creationism and when life begins. The bottom line is that

Terzian cannot have it both ways. He cannot at will lay claim to a property as the "discoverer," according to the doctrine of discovery, as did the Europeans, and at the same time agree with the Bering Strait proposition as do many Americans. The first proposes that no one was here, so the land "naturally" belonged to Europeans. The second supports the idea that people were here long before the Europeans arriving through the Bering Straits theory (one of several migration theories) and ignoring what the first Americans believe: "the People" have occupied this land since the beginning of time. If Terzian was consistent, he would thus have to conclude that Indians are the rightful owners of this land and of their ancestors' bones. He just cannot bring himself to do this because it is easier to form ill-informed perspectives, particularly because these *notions* fit his sensibilities well; or possibly as Upton Sinclair so famously stated about the information he provided in his book *the Jungle*, "It is difficult to get a man to understand something, when his salary depends on his not understanding it." History has shown that it has not been in the economic interest of Americans to understand the religions of Indians or any interpretation of their indigenous perspectives.

The few policies like NAGPRA that Indians have been able to shape in their own interests naturally rub Terzian, archaeologists, and casino owners like Donald Trump the wrong way—and rightfully so. Federal Indian legislation is rooted in the *domestic dependent nation* status, which was inspired by the supposedly benevolent federal government that defined itself as the "trustee" of Indian land. It has been stated in earlier chapters that Euro-Americans define land as giving them increased freedoms, freedoms that could have been acquired only by increasing their land base. For land-based religious people like American Indians, NAGPRA protects not only their religion but also the very essence of who they are.

Another example that supports the importance of NAGPRA is the manufactured "land dispute" between the Hopi and the Navajo People. Had this disputed land not been filled with coal, uranium, and water, it is doubtful that the federal government would have intervened and relocated approximately 5,000 Navajo and 100 Hopi elders "for their own protection." There is no doubt that the Navajo population outgrew their land base and infringed on Hopi land. However, information from the traditional people suggests the two Indian nations wanted to work out this issue within their respective tribes. It was clear from the beginning that once the removal of Indians from the disputed area was complete, Peabody Coal

Company would move in to remove the coal from the earth and in the process destroy numerous sacred sites and petroglyphs, or rock art as Americans call them. This land dispute is not a coincidence. It was manufactured in order to benefit large corporate interests.

It is important to ask how different is the removal of the Navajo and the Hopi people from the removal of the Cherokee in 1830? If students do not know about the first removal of Indians they might not be able to make the connection between the historical dance of yesterday with the federal treatment of Indians today or speculate about future removals.

The Navajo/Hopi case demonstrates the power of new actors: corporate actors, while the actors for the removal of the Cherokee people were states, Georgia specifically. While in both cases Indians were removed, the interests of corporations and of states are very much aligned. Nonetheless, Americans usually understand and often accept that the federal government has the power to remove people, Indian or non-Indian, through *eminent domain*. However, what keeps the federal government from just relocating Indians without justifying or rationalizing their actions may have a lot to do with the tension that exists between our political and economic systems. It might also be as Native scholar Elizabeth Cook-Lynn so succinctly states, namely, that Americans have a moral dilemma, "which for Americans mean that there are many conflicting versions of what is thought to be "decent and/or moral" (2001, 52).

> What America wants in its race relations with American Indians is to steal and occupy land, to kill and otherwise destroy the land's inhabitants, and yet provide an ethical example throughout the world of a democratic and "good" society developed for the purpose of profiting from that activity.

To demonstrate this moral dilemma, Cook-Lynn cites Joe Marshall's essay *On Behalf of the Wolf*, that shows Indians and wolves have faced similar difficulties. "Wolves have not served the agrarian interests of an economic system based on domestication, just as the Indian's failure to disappear has not served the national myth" (2001, 55).

Because Indians have not disappeared and because Indians continue to expose the contradictions apparent in federal Indian legislation, tribes are often forced to seek more benign forms of economic development as a possible solution to their economic woes. As was previously pointed out, Indians have been gambling since before the Europeans arrived. Back then, Indian gaming was not allowed in the same way Indians were not permitted to have giveaways or practice many of their ceremonies and traditions (see Chapter 3). Furthermore, as the Reagan Administration began cutting federal funding to Indians, he also encouraged Indians to develop plans that would solve their economic woes and get them off the "federal dole." That is why in 1986, the Mashantucket Pequot Tribe of Ledyard, Connecticut, with a population of 350, opened a twenty-one hundred seat bingo hall. Then six years later, in 1992, they opened Foxwood high stakes bingo and casino. What is all the more interesting is that the Pequot Tribe was not even a federally recognized tribe in 1983. In 1970, a man of Pequot descent led the effort for the federal recognition of the Pequot Tribe. The government officially recognized the tribe in 1983.

Thus, it is the politicization of Indians and the tactical responses of tribal governments to the federal government that shapes Indian politics and opens up new relationships. To what extent the Indian Gaming Regulatory Act (IGRA) furthers the survival or elimination of tribal nations is still unknown. However, no one could have predicted the magnitude of the events that unfolded after the passage of the IGRA. In 1988, when the IGRA became law, revenues from Indian gaming, mostly from bingo, were only $100 million. Within fifteen years, tribal revenue increased to $16.7 billion, 60 percent of which was generated by 20 tribal casinos (Mason 2000). While most of the tribes have used their gaming revenues wisely, some have also used this resource to play "dirty" politics as was done in two tribes in Louisiana.

In the summer of 2005, the U.S. Senate Indian Affairs Committee began investigating the payment of $82 million by Indian tribes to lobbyist Jack Abramoff and public affairs executive Michael Scanlon. One of Abramoff's clients was the Louisiana Coushatta tribe, which gave the money to Abramoff in hopes of blocking approval of a competing casino project in Louisiana by the Jena Band of Choctaws. According to published reports, in their efforts to stop the Jena Band from having gaming on their reservation, the Coushatta contributed $50,000 to a conservative interest group in 2001 and $100,000 in 2002 (Casinowatch.org).

The above example demonstrates that as the revenues of the tribes increase, so does their capacity to play politics and infringe upon the level of sovereignty of other tribes as well. These types of tactics have been very disconcerting to many Indian nations. This is one of the reasons many tribes are against Indian gaming on their land. There is a belief among many traditional Indians that money may not only provide the much-needed revenue for the tribe, but indeed has the capacity to corrupt.

Similar to gaming, the struggle for American Indians to protect sacred sites and to have access to them for traditional ceremonies and rituals has been a hotly debated issue. For example, some Native nations requested that specific areas defined as sacred sites be off limits to people during a period when this area is in need of rejuvenation. At some of these sacred sites, rock climbers and other tourists were asked to voluntarily not use the area during a specific month. Many Americans recognized the importance of not entering this area during this period and respected the tribe's wishes. Others protested the closure and refused to respect the request of the Native peoples. Rock climbing businesses and those businesses attracting tourists refused to honor the tribe's requests, citing that they had every right to stay open.

There are three examples of sacred sites currently being threatened. One is the Medicine Wheel in Wyoming, which is sacred to many tribes in Montana, Wyoming, Oklahoma, and South Dakota. Another one is Mt Graham in Arizona. The third one is Badger Two Medicine in Montana, where oil drilling would destroy a sacred area used by Blackfeet and other tribes. More recently, other debates have surfaced, such as snow making for ski areas on many mountains defined as sacred by Natives.

Unfortunately, while tribal governments must often rely on the actions of the federal government and decisions of the Supreme Court to protect the limited rights they are allowed to exercise, tribal governments will continue appealing to the federal government as that is all they can do. After all, the federal government defined itself as the legal guardian of Indians. It seems only fair that the federal government therefore fulfill its mission as the "protectorate" of Indian people.

Tribal governments, by choice or by circumstances, are often not included in the constitutional order of the United States. The fact that tribal governments are rooted in the status of *domestic dependent nations* ensures that a high level of complexity and ambiguity will continue when creating Indian legislation. Whether a consequence of time, increased negotiating skills of tribes, a more flexible federal government, or through Indian activism, tribes have been able to create systems that continue to seek the interests of its members.

However, it is doubtful that the survival of tribal governments would have occurred had its members not created a strong tribal identity. Identity politics is not a new phenomenon. In its simplest form, identity politics is how a person, or in this case a tribe, sees politics, and with what lens politics is viewed and understood. To several Americans, to identify oneself through heritage, language, customs, rituals, similar to how tribal nationalists do, is un-American. This is seen as transferring allegiance from a political identity (American) to a cultural identity (Lakota and so forth). Traditional tribal governments and other less Americanized groups contribute to a tenuous political identity and thus pay less tribute to the accepted national political identity created by the federal government.

We know the sole purpose of Indian legislation was to change the cultural identity of Indians from being a collective with a special relationship to land to an American where property is owned privately and exploited. Through the Reorganization Act of 1930, tribal governments were supposed to impose identities and downplay any cultural relevancy and what it may have meant to be Native within the context of being American. It was hoped that American Indians, Indigenous Peoples, and so forth, would shed any cultural identity that had bonded them for centuries and willingly accept what it means to be American.

To traditional Indians or tribal Indians, to be *Indian* is a cultural identity not necessarily separate from but inclusive of politics, religion, and land. With the introduction of ownership of land, and the refusal to allow Indians to practice their religion, the first of many identity crises for Indians began to form. Therefore, what it means to be Indian for tribally enrolled and politically active members has a greater capacity to form a political lens that skews American Indian history in favor of Indigenous peoples in the same way American history is skewed to favor the first immigrants.

Consequently, tribal governments and members worked not only to discard previous images of Indians, but in the process exposed the true nature of the federal government, eventually facilitating the creation of a new identity, one that was more relative to the experience of Indians. They realized it was important to construct an image of their collectiveness than what was being portrayed. These imposed Euro-American images would need to be shattered and replaced by a more respectful and historically correct image created by the first People.

Therefore, it is the relationship between images, situations, and policies that is of importance. The political identity of what it means to be (American) Indian has, on many Indian nations, been replaced with an identity based on tribal nationalism. In addition, while tribal governments continue to sustain a government that is more just and kinder than the one they were forced to emulate, the U.S. Government continues to create Indian legislation, rooted in the *domestic dependent nation* status, and certainly ambiguous and fictitious at best. Consequently, when examining the transition of the other American governments from dependency to sovereignty, we must be prepared to be consistently confused and understand federal Indian legislation as the fictitious instrument of control it really is. The diverse actors, coupled with diverse interests, therefore continue to make *The Other American Governments* a provocative and stimulating area of research.

BIBLIOGRAPHY

Akwesasne Notes, Summer 1987.

Beck, Peggy, Anna Lee Walters, and Nia Francisco. *The Sacred: Ways of Knowledge, Sources of Life* Tsaile, Arizona: Navajo Community College Press, 1996.

Brennan, William Justice. Lyng v. Northwest Indian Cemetery Protective Association, 485 U.S. 439, 460 1988.

Button, James W. *Black Violence*, New Jersey: Princeton University Press, 1978.

Bureau of Indian Affairs 1891, Circular No. 1665, Indian Dancing, American Indian Historian, Vol. 8, No. 3:43-44

Churchill, Ward and Glenn T. Morris, Key Indian Laws and Cases" *The State of Native America.* ed. M. Annette Jaimes. Boston: South End Press, 1992.

Churchill, Ward. *From a Native Son.* Boston: South End Press, 1996.

Cohen, Felix. *Handbook of Federal Indian Law*. Albuquerque: University of New Mexico Press, 1942.

Conrad, Geoffrey W. and Arthur A. Demarest. *Religion and Empire*. Cambridge: Cambridge University Press, 1984.

Cook-Lynn, Elizabeth. *Why I Can't Read Wallace Stegner and other Essays*. Madison: University of Wisconsin Press, 1996.

Cook-Lynn, Elizabeth. *Anti-Indian in Modern America*. Chicago: University of Illinois Press, 2001.

Cook-Lynn, Elizabeth. *New Indians, Old Wars.* Chicago: University of Illinois Press, 2007.

Cornell, Stephen. *The Return of the Native*. New York: Oxford University Press, 1988.

Deloria,Vine, Jr. "Religion and the Modern American Indian." *Current History*, Dec 1974.

Deloria, Vine, Jr. "Trouble in High Places: Erosion of American Indian Rights to Religious freedom in the United States" *The State of Native America*. ed. M. Annette Jaimes. Boston: South End Press, 1992.

Deloria, Vine, Jr. "The Distinctive Status of Indian Rights," *The Plains Indians of the Twentieth Century*, ed. Peter Iverson. Norman: University of Oklahoma Press, 1985.

Deloria, Vine, Jr. and Clifford Lyttle. *American Indians, American Justice*. Texas: University of Texas Press, l983.

Dorsen, Norman, President ACLU, ed. *The Rights of Indians and Tribes.* Carbondale Illinois: Southern Illinois University Press, 1992.

duPreez, Peter. *The Politics of Identity*. Oxford: Basil Blackwell Publishers, 1980.

Elstain, Jean Bethke. *Democracy on Trail*. New York: Basic Books, 1995.

Erdoes, Richard. *The Sun Dance People*, New York: Alfred A. Knopf, 1972.

Fenton, William N., ed. *Parker on the Iroquois*, Syracuse: Syracuse University Press, 1968.

Fleming, Walter C. *The Complete Idiot's Guide to Native American History*, New York: Penguin, 2003.

Forbes, Jack. *Native Americans and Nixon*. Los Angeles: University of California, 1981.

Foreman, Grant. *Indian Removal: The Emigration of the Five Civilized Tribes of Indians*. Norman: University of Oklahoma Press, l953.

Gates, Paul W. *The Rape of Indian Land*. New York: Arno Press, 1979.

Getches, D.H., C.F. Wilkinson, and R.A. Williams Jr. *Federal Indian Law, Cases and Materials*, St. Paul: West Publishing, 1993.

Grinde, Donald A., Jr. and Bruce Johansen. *Exemplar of Liberty*. Los Angeles: American Indian Studies Center, University of California, 1991.

Grinde, Donald A. Jr. *The Iroquois and the Founding of the America.* San Francisco: Indian Historian Press, 1977.

Hassig, Ross. *War and Society in Ancient Mesoamerica.* Berkeley: University of California Press, 1992.

Hertzberg, Hazel. "Reaganomics on the Reservation" *The New Republic*, November 22, 1982, 63.

Hirschfelder, Arlene and Martha Kreipe de Montano. *The American Almanac.* New York: Prentice Hall, 1993.

Huntington, Samuel. *Political Order in Changing Societies.* New Haven: Yale University Press, 1968.

Jaimes, M. Annette and Theresa Harley. "American Indian Women" in *The State of Native America*. ed. M. Annette Jaimes. Boston: South End Press, 1992.

Johansen, Bruce. *The Forgotten Founders*. Massachusetts: Gambit, 1982.

Johansen, Bruce and Roberto Maestas. *Wasi'chu, The Continuing Indian Wars*. New York: Monthly Review Press, 1979.

Jones, Maldwyn Allen. *American Immigration*. Chicago: University of Chicago Press, 1992.

Josephy, Alvin M. Jr. *Red Power: The American Indians' Fight for Freedom*. New York: McGraw Hill, 1971.

Kelly, Lawrence C. *The Navajo Indians and Federal Policy*. Arizona: University of Arizona Press, 1968.

Kelly, G.A. *The Psychology of Personal Constructs*. New York: Norton, 1955.

Levitan, Sar A. and Barbara Hetrick. *Big Brother's Indian Programs*. New York: McGraw-Hill, 1971.

Limmerick, Patricia Nelson. *The Legacy of Conquest: The Unbroken Past of the American West* New York: W. W. Norton, 1987.

Lipset, Seymore. *American Exceptionalism: A Double-edged Sword*. New York: Norton, 1996.

Lokken Ray Jr. ed. *Meet Dr. Franklin*. Philadelphia: Franklin Institute, 1981.

Mama Amina. "Sheroes and Villains: Conceptualizing Colonial and Contemporary Violence Against Women in Africa," in J. Jacqui Alexander and Chandra Talpade Mohanty (eds). *Feminist Genealogies, Colonial Legacies, Democratic Future*. New York: Routledge Press, 1997.

Mason, Dale W. *Indian Gaming, Tribal Sovereignty and American Politics*. Norman: University of Oklahoma Press, 2000.

Matthiessen, Peter. *In the Spirit of Crazy Horse*. New York: Penguin Books, 1992.

McAdam Doug. *Political Process and the Development of Black Insurgency*. Chicago: University of Chicago Press, 1982.

Menchú, Rigoberta, I. *Rigoberta Menchú: An Indian Woman in Guatemala*. New York: Verso, 1983.

Mihesuah, Devon A. *American Indians: Stereotypes & Realities*. Atlanta: Clarity Press, 1996.

Mohawk, John ed. *Exiled in the Land of the Free*. Santa Fe: Clear Light , 1991.

Monsen, Frederick. "Festivals of the Hopi: Religion, the Inspiration, and Dancing, an Expression of Their National Ceremonies," in *The Craftsmen*, No. 12. 1907.

New York Times Index 1950 – 1985.

O'Brien, Sharon. *American Indian Tribal Governments*. Norman and London: University of Oklahoma Press, 1989.

Olson, James, and Raymond Wilson. *Native Americans in the Twentieth Century*. Chicago: University of Illinois, l984.

Ortiz, Alfonzo. *The Tewa World: Space, Time, Beings, and Becoming in a Pueblo Society*. Chicago: University of Chicago Press, 1969.

Ortiz, Alfonzo. "*Look to the Mountaintop*" in *Essays on Reflection*. Graham Ward, ed. Boston: Houghton Mifflin, 1973.

Ortiz, Roxanne D. *Indians of the Americas: Human Rights and Self Determination*. London: Zed Press, 1984.

Parker, Arthur C. *The Constitution of the Five Nations*. Albany: State Museum, 1916.

Parker, Arthur C. *Red Jacket: Last of the Seneca*. New York: McGraw-Hill, 1952.

Parker, Arthur C. *Parker On the Iroquois*, ed. William N. Fenton. Syracuse: Syracuse University Press, 1968.

Pevar, Stephen L. *The Rights of Indians and Tribes*. Carbondale: Southern Illinois University Press, 1992.

Petoskey, John. "Indians and the First Amendment". *American Indian Policy in the Twentieth Century* ed Vine Deloria, Jr. Norman: University of Oklahoma, 1985.

Piven, Frances Fox and Richard Cloward. *The Poor People's Movement*. New York: Random House, 1978.

Popkin, Samuel L. *The Rational Peasant*. Berkeley: University of California, 1979.

Rostow, W. W. *The Stages of Economic Growth, a Non-Communist Manifesto*. Cambridge: Cambridge University Press, 1962.

Schmidt, Ryan W. "American Indian Identity and Blood Quantum in the 21st Century: A Critical Review." *Journal of Anthropology* 2011, 1–9.

Scott, James C. *The Moral Economy of the Peasant*. New Haven: Yale University, 1976.

Silman, Janet. *Enough is Enough: Aboriginal Women Speak Out*. Ontario: Women's Press, 1987.

Steiner, Stan. *New Indians*. New York: Harper & Row Publishers, 1968

Taylor, Charles. *Multiculturalism and the Politics of Recognition*. New Jersey: Princeton University Press. 1992.

Thompson J. Eric S. *The Rise and Fall of Maya Civilization*. Norman: Oklahoma Press, 1963.

Tucker, Robert C. *The Marx-Engels Reader*. New York: W.W. Norton, 1978.

Versluis, Arthur. *Native American Traditions*. Boston: Element Books, 1993.

Wagner, Sally Roesch. *Sisters in Spirit: Iroquois Influence on Early Feminists*. Summertown, Tennessee: Native Voices. 2001.

Wallace, Paul. *The White Roots of Peace*. Long Island: Ira J. Friedman, 1946.

Wax, Murray L. and Robert W. Buchanan, eds. *Solving "The Indian Problem:" The White Man's Burdensome Business*. New York: New York Times Book, 1975.

Wax, Murray L. *Indian-Americans: Unity & Diversity*. New Jersey: Prentice Hall, 1971.

Watson, Mary Ann and Oneida Meranto. *The Changing American Indians in a Changing America: Video-Cases of American Indian Peoples*. New Jersey: Prentice Hall, 2001.

Weatherford, Jack. *Indian Givers.* New York: Ballantine Books, 1988.

Weber, Max. 1904 "The Protestant Ethic and the Spirit of Capitalism," *Essays in Sociology*. ed H.H. Gerth and C. Wright Mills. Oxford Press, 1948.

Weyler, Rex. *Blood of the Land*. New York: Vintage Books, 1982.

Wilkins, David E. *American Indian Politics and the American Political System*. Boulder: Rowman & Littlefield, 2002.

Wilkins, David E. and Heidi Kiiwetinepinesiik Stark. *American Indian Politics and the American Political System*. Boulder: Rowman & Littlefield Publishers, 2011.

Wilkinson, Charles, and Eric Biggs. "The Evolution of the Termination Policy." *American Indian Law Review 5* no. 1 (1977): 43.

Witt, Shirley, and Stan Steiner. *The Way: An Anthology of American Indian Literature.* New York: Alfred A. Knopf, 1972.

Zimmerman, Larry J., and Brian Leigh Molyneaux. *Native North America.* Norman: University of Oklahoma Press, 1996.

INTERVIEWS AND PRESENTATIONS

Lew Gurwitz, Lawyer for Native American issues, October 6, 1987, and June 17, 1986.

Bill Means, Native American activist, November 25, 1987, and March 11, 1986.

Russell Means, Native American activist, AIM member October 17, 1988.

Vernon Bellecourt, Native American activist, AIM member, December 2, 1987 and March 20 1986.

John Echohawk, Lawyer for the National Rights Fund (NARF) September 1988.

Dr. Charles Wilkinson, Professor of Law, University of Colorado, July 11, 1991.

Peter MacDonald, Ivan Sidney, and Hollis Whitson, *"The Land Dispute, and Myths of the Land Dispute."* Address given at University of Colorado, Boulder. November 19, 1986.

INDEX

United States
   laissez-faire (hands-off)
   government, 4
U.S. Commission on Civil Rights, 27
U.S. Constitution, 20
   Amendment 10, 5
   and Great Law of Peace,
   structural similarities
   between, 19
U.S. Federal Government, 20
U.S. Senate Indian Affairs Committee,
   123

V
Viejas Tribe, 103
Violence Against Women's Act of
   2012, 117–118

W
War on Poverty, 52
WARN. *See* Women of All Red Nations
   (WARN)
Warren Court, 102
Warrior, Clyde, 92
Watkins, Arthur V., 49–50
Watson, Mary Ann, ix
Weatherford, Jack, 24
Weber, Max, 61
Wheelock, Eleazer, 73
Wilkenson, David, xi
Wilkins, David E., xi, 77
Wilkinson, Charles, 51
Wilson, Dick, 2, 12, 119

Women of All Red Nations (WARN),
   109
Women's Movement, viii, 88
Worldview, defined, 27–28

Y
Yakima, 18, 22, 98

Z
Zinn, Howard, vii
Zuni, 28

CPSIA information can be obtained
at www.ICGtesting.com
Printed in the USA
FSOW02n0221260817
37948FS